Journey Toward Renewal

To my wife, Colleen Nelson, and our children, Will, Debbie, and David, who continue to be constructive critics in the process of my becoming a more mature person.

To my wife, Dorothy Lincoln, and our daughter, Christine, who allowed me the freedom to be wrong in my search for the right.

Journey Toward Renewal

WILLIAM R. NELSON
WILLIAM F. LINCOLN

JUDSON PRESS, Valley Forge

JOURNEY TOWARD RENEWAL

Foreword

The church is renewable. This is the central thesis of this admirable book by Bill Nelson and Bill Lincoln. But it is far more than a thesis. It is a conclusion drawn from five years of experimenting in a prestigious church in Rochester, New York, that methodically went about the process of evaluating its situation in the inner city and took steps that were appropriate to it.

Written not to inspire but to explain, these chapters tell how any similar church can implement change both within its own congregation and in the surrounding community.

Lake Avenue Baptist Church is a church with a distinguished history that has seen its neighborhood deteriorate and its members move to the suburbs. Like many such churches it has had to ask hard questions about its reason for existence, and plot a new course in keeping with the times. That it was able to do so with the minimum of disruption to the stability of an ongoing congregational life is a tribute to its pastoral leadership and the forces that converged to bring significant change.

Here is careful documentation of the hazards of change, and the difficulties. Here too is recognition of the incompleteness and temporariness of the results. But woven through the story is evidence that a congregation can rise to the challenge facing it and that individual members can find a new depth of Christian faith in doing so.

I am especially struck by the analogy to the automobile that shapes the form of this story and by the practical "Guidelines for Group Discussion" at the end of the book. What Nelson and Lincoln have left us of their experience at Lake Avenue could well serve as a manual for study and exploration by inner-city churches across America.

WALDEN HOWARD
Editor, FAITH/AT/WORK Magazine

Acknowledgements

This collaboration is a case study of the search for renewal in the institutional church from a personal perspective. It does not attempt to tell the whole story; it merely presents the understanding and at times the bias of the coauthors. Both are indebted to many people whose insights and interpretations are incorporated in the finished book.

Nelson's gratitude goes to Ray S. Kicklighter, the renewal strategist of the Lake Avenue Baptist Church, whose friendship was a quiet center throughout the five years. He is also grateful to Milton C. Froyd, former Dean of Colgate Rochester Divinity School, whose counsel was invaluable throughout the experiment. His appreciation is also expressed to Harvey A. Everett and E. B. Hicks of the American Baptist Home Mission Societies, whose support was a model of pastoral concern for the entire family. Many others were instrumental in contributing to his growth, such as Trevor and Liz Ewell, Richard and Marian Johanknecht, and the four couples in the Bible study group which met every other Tuesday evening.

Lincoln would like to acknowledge the personal support of William Schneider, a Roman Catholic suburbanite who was involved in WEDGE from the beginning and became its first interim director. He is also grateful to Jenette Valdez, the primary indigenous leader of Brown Square, who became the first residential executive director of WEDGE. His appreciation is also extended to Paul Thayer of the Lake Avenue Baptist Church who moved from the suburbs to reside in Brown Square and became the energetic associate director of WEDGE. Many others gave of themselves freely in the difficult role of nonresidents, such as Robert Mahone, Vernon Thayer, Norma Stoneham, Liz Ewell, Daisy Fleming, William T. Bluhm, and Richard Bresson.

The manuscript has been helped by editorial suggestions made by Harold L. Twiss of Judson Press. A special word of thanks goes to Nelson's secretary, Willabelle Parker, for typing the final manuscript. The book could not have been completed without the encouragement of Harold W. Richardson, Executive Secretary of the American Baptist Board of Education and Publication, and J. E. Dollar, Resident Director of the American Baptist Assembly, Green Lake, Wisconsin. It is presented as a contribution to the new thrust of program development at Green Lake which is aimed at stimulating the process of renewal in local churches.

WILLIAM R. NELSON

March 1, 1971
Green Lake, Wisconsin.

Contents

Introduction

Both people and institutions can change. God works through individuals and corporate structures to accomplish his ministry of reconciliation in the world. The institution which he has chosen as the main vehicle for communicating what he has done for all men through Christ is the church. Yet the structures of the church are often introverted and self-centered. Most church leaders are prepared to deal with this kind of problem at the personal level, but the transition is rarely made to the process of institutional change.

The basic difficulty is that we have chosen to major on inspiration, to minor on fellowship, and to avoid follow-through. The process of institutional change is the science of follow-through. From the very smallest beginning a vision embodied in a few searching individuals can be the beginning of new life for even a strong and successful church.

A few single young adults from the Lake Avenue Baptist Church in Rochester, New York, attended a Recreation Lab at the American Baptist Assembly in Green Lake, Wisconsin, during the summer of 1955. Few people realized that their presence at Green Lake marked a very inconspicuous turning point in the history of the church. This book is the story of a chain reaction which took place because they decided to follow through on the vision that they received in 1955.

What started as a timid recreational program for neighborhood children led to a full-scale experiment in church renewal from 1965 to 1970. The church was chosen for the experiment by the American Baptist Home Mission Societies because of the evidence of follow-through which had already been demonstrated during the previous ten years.

The experiment itself accelerated the process of institutional change more rapidly than usual so that it could be examined as a resource for other congregations. The pain and joy of this struggle will serve as a reminder that a religious institution is subject to the strengths and weaknesses of its corporate membership as are all social institutions. The presence of human frailty in such abundance reaffirms the necessity of trusting God for guidance as new directions emerge.

This book is written for lay and clergy leaders who want to be used by God as change agents within traditional churches. The only requirements for entering into this process of institutional change are the persistence to follow through and the willingness to risk failure. It is expected that your experience will be different from that of the coauthors. Yet a few of the steps in the process will likely be the same. A brief summary of the major developments in the experiment will help you to identify those areas of similarity to your situation.

Chapter 1 provides an overview of the personal struggle of two leaders in the experiment who were initially in the driver's seat. Both men entered into the process as aggressive change agents who were determined to bring about renewal in the institutional church through their own engineering skill. Their actual involvement with people resulted in a shift from a manipulative, program-oriented approach to a more responsive, person-centered approach. They viewed their new freedom as taking hands off the steering wheel of the project and moving to the enabling, resource position of backseat driving.

Chapter 2 describes the preliminary phase of the process of institutional change which received a fresh start in 1955. The responsiveness of the congregation to the urban challenge paved the way for a more self-conscious design for renewal. The new model which was projected included calling a free-lance minister in 1965 whose only responsibility was to be a resource for the experiment.

Chapter 3 describes the difficulty that the church had in gearing into an expanded community ministry during the first year of the actual experiment. Following a six-month period of research, the initiative for change came from an ecumenical team of clergy. The new thing which emerged was a neighborhood association. It brought several church groups together to respond to the needs of their common community.

Chapter 4 depicts the record-breaking speed with which an ecumenical approach to community ministry developed during the next two years. The new ecumenical programs for children, youth, and adults provided many opportunities for lay leader development. The need for better coordination and for lay participation at the decision-making level led to the formation of a sector-wide organization for promoting ecumenical ministry.

Chapter 5 describes an unexpected detour off the main highway of ecumenical cooperation to the back streets of a forgotten inner-city community. The needs of neighboring residents had been previously unknown to the majority of suburban-oriented church members.

Chapter 6 describes the collision courses which resulted from two contrasting approaches to urban mission. During the process of developing new forms of ecumenical ministry, the churches became identified with property owners who had a vested interest in preserving their neighborhood. These property values became a barrier to effective ministry with welfare recipients in general and with different minority groups in particular. The motivation behind the prevailing ecumenical approach was challenged by welfare recipients and tenants who insisted upon being treated as people in their own right.

Chapter 7 documents the ensuing tension during the third and fourth years of the experiment which resulted in the high speed traffic on the main highway of ecumenical cooperation yielding the right-of-way to the poor. An unanticipated side of mission was the way in which a deteriorating neighborhood gave an affluent congregation new insights about the reality of urban pluralism and the appropriateness of nonresidents relating to the inner city through a supportive role.

Chapter 8 relates a growing awareness of the necessity for refueling on the part of involved persons who were moving out on either of the new routes to community ministry. The cultivation of small-group ministry enabled some church members to find a base of supportive community which helped to sustain them in further mission involvement. Others found these small groups to be a source of personal enrichment which enabled them to seek out new ways of expressing their Christian faith in action.

Chapter 9 deals with the actual process of institutional change in the church itself during the fifth year of the experiment. A long-range planning committee was designated through official channels in order to determine the church's priorities for ministry during the next five years. This process of strategic planning helped to consolidate the gains of the previous four years and to self-consciously mark the route for the future.

Chapter 10 describes the continuing momentum which persisted beyond the formal limits of the five-year experiment. Since renewal is viewed as a process of becoming, the period of testing comes to an end so that the new insights can be expressed in more effective ways. As if the project were starting again, staff changes were made with more clearly defined objectives and a real sense of direction.

Many books about church renewal leave the reader confused because of the great gap between his actual situation and various highly developed models which seem unattainable. This account will start where most churchmen are, that is, struggling to find relevant ministry by routinely participating in a variety of traditional activities within a church which at least superficially projects an image of success. It is written for clergy and laity who have the uncomfortable feeling that something is missing in their church. To show what it is, how it can be discovered, and where it will lead has already been hinted at in outline form. In a sense each church will be able to fill in the details according to the unique characteristics of its particular setting. Yet it may be helpful to know more about the inner workings of a process of institutional change as it was lived out by the members of a rather typical urban church.

This book is written with the strong conviction that renewal is closely associated with the growth and change observable in people and in institutions. Consequently, cross references will be minimized in favor of personal observations and analyses of specific situations which are not unlike many others throughout the nation. As the two staff members most closely associated with the project share their experience, it is hoped that the reader will be confronted with the inescapable truth that "renewal begins with me." May the experience of the coauthors serve as an encouragement for you to continue following through even when the outcome is not clear.

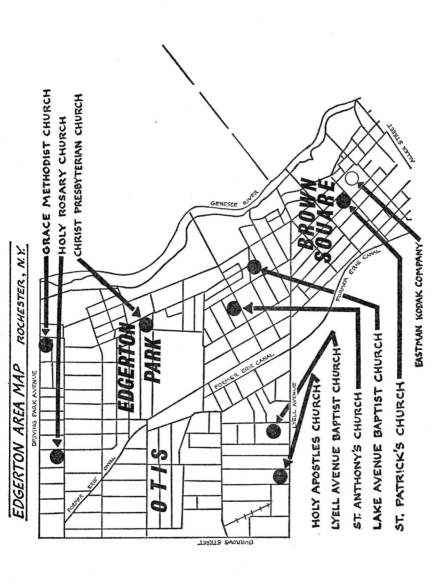

EDGERTON AREA MAP *ROCHESTER, N.Y.*

GRACE METHODIST CHURCH
HOLY ROSARY CHURCH
CHRIST PRESBYTERIAN CHURCH

DRIVING PARK AVENUE

GENESEE RIVER

BROWN SQUARE

ALLEN STREET

FORMER ERIE CANAL

EDGERTON PARK

FORMER ERIE CANAL

OTIS

FORMER ERIE CANAL

LYELL AVENUE

BURROWS STREET

HOLY APOSTLES CHURCH
LYELL AVENUE BAPTIST CHURCH
ST. ANTHONY'S CHURCH
LAKE AVENUE BAPTIST CHURCH
ST. PATRICK'S CHURCH
EASTMAN KODAK COMPANY

Looking Ahead to Chapter 1

The personal pilgrimage of the coauthors during the five-year experiment provides an inside view of the renewal process. Their respective involvement in the congregation and in the community helped them to overcome their "one-man-show" orientation to the ministry. The way in which key lay persons accepted them and responded to their concerns short-circuited aggressive, organizational syndromes and opened the door to responsive, enabling ministries. The new relationships between clergy and laity which they experienced created a new expectation for other members of the church's ministerial staff. This overview of the renewal process in chapter 1 describes the most effective role for clergymen as that of "Backseat Driving."

1   Backseat Driving

"One of the main blocks to the renewal of the Church is the clergyman who does not trust God enough to allow the laity to be ministers too." [1] This startling conclusion was reached by William Nelson as a result of his own experience near the midpoint of the five-year experiment in the Lake Avenue Baptist Church of Rochester, New York. It reflected a drastic shift in his understanding of the ministry. He no longer thought of himself as the central figure through whom everyone communicated and from whom all important decisions emanated. Limiting the renewal process to his style and vision was finally overcome as the validity of lay ministry was recognized and affirmed.

This struggle involved several key persons. One was a layman who cared enough about one of his ministers to accept him as a friend and at the same time to bombard him with a persistent anticlergy bias. The result of this close relationship was a thawing of the invisible wall which traditionally separates most clergy and laity. This would not have happened if his minister had remained aloof by hiding behind the mask of "treating all people alike." *Every pastor needs a few close friends in order to be truly human.* The danger of showing favoritism usually eliminates this kind of openness with lay people. Feelings of competition often get in the way of this kind of freedom with fellow ministers. Yet one of the hardest lessons for a pastor to learn is the ability to receive love from those who are allowed to become trusted friends. It is much easier to follow the more customary pattern of giving love to those who need his warm affirmation.

---

[1] William R. Nelson, "I'm Learning to Take 'Hands Off,' " *Faith at Work* Magazine (Summer, 1969), p. 4. Reprinted with permission in Bruce Larson and Ralph Osborne's *The Emerging Church* (Waco, Texas: Word, Incorporated, 1970), pp. 125-129.

Another person who got inside Nelson's life was a fellow minister who began as an urban trainee under his supervision and emerged as a co-leader of the experiment. William F. Lincoln had his own special activist style of ministry, but inwardly it was the same aggressive, manipulating approach which Nelson had developed. The gradual coming together of these two men and their overcoming the hidden barrier of competition which initially separated them is the background drama of the entire experiment.

Nelson and Lincoln eventually acquired the vision of becoming enabling ministers as a result of new relationships that they were establishing with key lay persons and with each other. Lincoln's strong point was social action, but the key to his success in the inner city was in the development of a new supportive role both for himself and for nonresidents from the Lake Avenue Church. Nelson's strong points were pastoral ministry and administration as he gradually shifted from a manipulative, organizational style of ministry to the more personal role of enabler. The two men described this process of personal growth in a joint presentation at the American Baptist Assembly in Green Lake, Wisconsin, on August 1, 1970.[2] Their perception of each other provided an added dimension of reality and honesty to the discussion.

LINCOLN: "Nelson is one man who enjoys his theological and academic credentials more than most people who possess the same titles. The Rev. Doctor does not hesitate disclosing to anyone that he pursued biblical studies in Germany and completed his graduate work at prestigious Princeton. On the other hand, he perpetuates a pride in having done his ministerial training in a pure seminary, Southern Baptist Theological Seminary of Louisville, which is grounded in fervent pietism and a strong biblical tradition. Thus, he plays both roles whenever one is more fitting than the other. Among liberals he is the professional theologian, while with conservatives he is the straight-laced good boy, a child of God who is awed with the amazing grace of Jesus Christ, his personal Lord and Savior. One might think that this is inconsistent, but not so when you realize he is an opportunist who is preoc-

[2] Excerpted from a tape recording made at the opening session of the Conference on the Church (sponsored by the Associated Homeland Ministries of the American Baptist Convention) under the leadership of the Rev. John A. Barker.

cupied with his own ego development.

"He also sees himself as an urban specialist. He has read a few of the right articles and likes to drop sociological terminology while walking around with planning maps visibly tucked under his arm. He thinks more of programs than he does of people. Still, however, socially he sometimes seems to be one of the few genuine people alive today.

"Nelson is a facade. He is also inflexible to adjust or even consider alternatives which are not of his making. He strives to surround people in structures of his choosing in order to control them. He is without doubt a manipulator, a dictator, a commander of a ship which he builds and forces others to sail. Why is it that all the right credentials—namely unquestionable scholarship and unique experience—are found in this man who is unreal and less than human? He is a lonely man who lives with a constantly gnawing insecurity that he and others will learn that he is something other than his self-image.

"That is how I would have introduced Nelson in the winter of 1965/66 after having known him for only four to six months. Today, in the summer of 1970, I would have to describe him quite differently."

NELSON: "It is gratifying to know that those who had a vision for the Lake Avenue Church also saw more in me than was apparent on the surface. I started off in 1965 playing a role and at the same time denying much of my past experience as a Southern Baptist because it was out of style in a city that was closely associated with the social gospel movement. It was natural to play to the new liberal audience and to forget that my past in the conservative South included a warm appreciation for such songs as 'Amazing Grace' and 'What a Friend We Have in Jesus.' This prayer meeting background from the South was denied for a while so that I could become a 'gung-ho' urban specialist. The only problem with this switch was that the new role just was not me. I did all the right things, like living in an Italian-American neighborhood with my family and working closely with all kinds of people in this changing community. Yet I knew that something was missing.

"My initial impression of Bill Lincoln was also not too

good. He enjoyed his reputation as the student body president of Franklin College in Indiana, and his Boston accent added color to his quiet but intensive voice. After earlier serving a small church in Indiana, he had been serving as a pastor for the previous year in the Bristol Hills area to the south of Rochester. Yet he readily admitted that he did not have the patience to sit down and listen to people. It even frustrated him to wait a few moments for someone to answer the telephone. This restless student at Colgate Rochester Divinity School was looking around for another assignment in an urban setting which would make better use of his boundless energy. He struck me right from the beginning as an impetuous activist and as the original angry young man. A social work inclination provided the center for his many interests, such as campus protest, poverty, housing, employment, and community organization. It used to bother me that his compulsive nature led him in five different directions at the same time. His grandiose schemes for social change seemed like impossible dreams. But his creative skill as a real urban specialist demanded many channels for expression.

"Since I was supposed to be his supervisor, we met each week during the first year for a tutorial seminar. We studied every possible aspect of community organization and urban renewal in relation to the particular needs of the immediate community around the Lake Avenue Church. A four-week advance course at the Urban Training Center for Christian Mission in Chicago had helped me to become acquainted with these new tools for public mission. As long as we were studying together, it went rather smoothly. Then the first clash came when Lincoln refused to run the Community Center for neighborhood children. At that point he really told me where to get off."

LINCOLN: "I was not only fighting you, but the entire church to which I was related as an urban trainee. To many people 'Lake Avenue' meant a forty-voice professional choir that sang Bach and Brahms on Sunday mornings. Lights flashed on and off in the vestibule to announce when Jesus was supposed to be present. This church has a tremendous budget and can do almost anything that it wants to do. It seemed to me that at the beginning of the experiment, 'Lake

Avenue' was trying to buy its way into urban mission by paying a lot of program bills and staying away from true involvement as far as possible.

"After a few months of working with neighborhood children, I went to Nelson's office and told him that I was through if this was the nature of our new urban experiment. Instead of throwing me out, he took me by the hand, led me to a nearby deteriorating community, and told me to 'get lost.' I was glad that I didn't have to bother any more with the institutional church and its ecclesiastical concerns.

"Now I was free to do my thing. It was hard and demanding. For a while it meant that I was separated from my wife Dorothy. I had gotten so far out of the church that there was a lot of personal conflict in my life. While I was searching for a way back, I also started watching Nelson change as he became more sensitive to the needs of people.

NELSON: "I had already taken a 'plunge' at the Urban Training Center for the purpose of sociological awareness, but a different kind of plunge was needed to free me from an authoritarian, organizational approach to the ministry. I got some help from a joyous group of people who were related to Faith at Work.[3] They loved me in spite of my manipulative tendencies. I sensed in them a style of life which was characterized by honesty and vulnerability. As I got to know them better, I learned that their strength came from acknowledging their weakness. My wife Colleen put her finger on the trouble while we were having lunch together during the course of a National Faith at Work Conference in New York City in January of 1968. She said rather bluntly: 'William, you are not running this conference; Bruce Larson is in charge.' I was just one of the sub-leaders who was so concerned about everything going just right that I couldn't relax for a minute. Colleen helped me to see that I was really running from myself—and God. Then it occurred to me that for the first

[3] A fellowship of men and women which crosses all barriers of nationality, church, race, and status to affirm that Jesus Christ is the Lord of all life and to work together for individual and corporate renewal. Growing out of the ministry of Episcopal priest Sam Shoemaker, this fellowship is held together by local, regional, and national conferences and publishes the *Faith at Work* Magazine, a Voice for the Emerging Church (297 Fifth Ave., New York, New York 10016).

time in recent years I had been invited to the conference primarily to talk about my personal Christian experience. It would no longer be possible to hide behind urban problems or biblical concepts. This realization was a new beginning in my life which made it possible for me to reclaim much of my past which had been buried in the South.

"During the course of the weekend conference I really learned to 'take hands off.' My small-group co-leader, viewed from my bias as a 'non-theological' housewife,[4] would not let me get away with controlling the group. I returned to Rochester from that 'upper room' at the Statler Hilton Hotel with a new perspective for my ministry. Upon further reflection the shift was like moving from the driver's seat where I was in control to the back seat where I was more concerned about affirming the real drivers, the laity."

LINCOLN: "It was during this time of ferment in Nelson's life that a deeper level of trust was developing between us. After two and a half years of competition and struggle, as if passing each other in the night, we finally made contact as two people who needed each other. From that point on, it was possible to allow each other to complement our acknowledged strengths and weaknesses. The new awareness that we started living out in the third and fourth years of the experiment was our own need for personal growth. Our struggle had to take place first before we dared to involve others in this kind of quest. Therefore, I started listening more intently to the needs of people in Brown Square as if I really cared about them. I no longer needed to use them as pawns in my grandiose scheme for total community renewal. At about the same time the focus of Nelson's ministry shifted to the cultivation of small-group life in the congregation."

NELSON: "I had been in a Bible study group for several years, but it was much more like an intellectual debating society than a sharing, supportive community. We used biblical concepts to test our understanding of truth and preferred

---

[4] William R. Nelson, "I'm Learning to Take 'Hands Off,' " *Faith at Work* Magazine (Summer, 1969), pp. 1-4, describes the painful experience in which a pastor learned the value of being ministered unto by a lay person as well as vice versa.

to discuss the Bible in a very abstract way. If this academic approach to the Bible was going to change, I decided that it would be better to demonstrate a more personal approach rather than just complain about our common intellectualizing tendency. I gradually learned how to share some of my experiences with this group. During the fifth year of our experiment, the entire group discovered a deeper relationship which made it possible for all to share on a more personal basis. At the same time I was observing Lincoln's new interest in the institutional church and his own willingness to take people more seriously."

LINCOLN: "It's embarrassing to talk about personal growth in the presence of my first Baptist pastor, Bob Slaughter,[5] who was instrumental in my decision to enter the ministry. At that time I just did not trust the church at all. I was very suspicious of the church and viewed it as fair game—an institution with a lot of resources that I could use. This is why I went 'secular' at first. Most of my fellow seminarians felt the same way, too. Then I finally realized that I had not given the church a fair chance. I balked at the real risk of ministry because of concern about my vested interest and my professional 'hang-ups.' It's possible to do a lot of damage to this God-given institution, but I'm thankful that we can never tear it down.

"The Lake Avenue Church had helped to initiate the Edgerton Area Neighborhood Association. One fault which I saw was the tendency for this community organization to be dominated by the churches that were behind it. An alternative approach called WEDGE emerged in Brown Square, over which tenants had control. The concept of WEDGE giving direction to the church was promoted to avoid an ecclesiastical 'take-over.' The Lake Avenue Church bought this approach and was accused of being noncooperative and unilateral. This unpopular role was reinforced by identifying with a Roman Catholic 'underground' church which also wanted to relate to WEDGE in a supportive role. This shifting style at 'Lake Avenue' made it possible for me to trust the church as an institution for the first time. Then it

---

[5] Rev. Robert E. Slaughter, who is currently serving as pastor of the Roselawn Community Baptist Church of Cincinnati, Ohio.

occurred to me that the church was an institution that could be renewed."

NELSON: "What I am just realizing is that the same thing that was happening in my life was also happening to the Lake Avenue Church. I was learning to take hands off my life instead of carefully controlling the extent to which I chose to risk myself. The same thing was happening to our church during this five-year experiment. An authentically mixed American community called Brown Square was also helping our church to take hands off the control of urban mission. This ecclesiastical shift from the driver's seat to a supportive role was quite different from the earlier organizational development phase aimed at getting people into church-sponsored projects. The new emphasis dealt with enabling persons to determine their own destinies. In other words, Lake Avenue was learning a new style of backseat driving just like I was experiencing at a more personal level.

"This kind of change does not come easily. Perhaps it is easier to discern in individuals than in institutions. Because God was working through a few persistent lay persons and a stubborn colleague in the ministry, I was able to break out of the role of play pretending to be an urban specialist, or even worse, a renewal expert. Then it was possible to reclaim my former heritage which emphasized personal commitment to Christ and to take this rediscovered faith with me in relating to the world. Now I find myself searching for new ways of serving the world from the perspective of a pastoral administrator. I am convinced more than ever that the gospel demands total commitment both to Christ *and* to the world."

LINCOLN: "I have become aware more recently of my tendency to alienate those who think differently than I do. I have been on all the right protest marches. I have signed all the right petitions. Then I finally got tired of harassing others and said that I wouldn't do it anymore. Now I realize how easy it is to develop stereotypes of people. For example, one of the groups that needs our ministry the most is the police force. At best we have had a 'duel-logue' instead of dialogue. We live in a pluralistic world and don't have the right to damn or judge anyone. Everybody doesn't have the same talents, interests, or priorities, but each has a contribution to make—even the little lady who reads to the blind person one hour a week or the person who just plays the piano for kids at Sunday school."

NELSON: "What has happened to Lincoln is my evidence that renewal has taken place at Lake Avenue. He is a man who combines the talent of Malcolm Boyd and Rod McKuen, a man who is learning to listen to people, a man who has imagination and ability to help poor people organize in order to more fully express themselves. I'm thankful for what he has taught me about involvement and for his patience in allowing me to be a growing person along with him. I have learned from him the beauty of creative conflict and how to profit from that kind of experience. We have had our share of conflict, but God used it to draw us closer to each other and to Him."

During the course of the five-year experiment both Nelson and Lincoln were moving toward being the persons they wanted to be. Nelson had learned that it did not help in the long run to act as though he was something that he really was not. He became more effective when he was able to listen acceptantly to himself, even to that part of his background which was "out of style" in Rochester. This new level of self-acceptance reduced the need for competition with Lincoln or defensiveness about his past. The result was a greater freedom to listen more acceptantly to others. This painful reorganization was the key "learning" from the experiment for Nelson.

Lincoln's initial hostility toward the institutional church was neutralized by the freedom that he was given to find himself in Brown Square. It was later overcome by Lake Avenue's acceptance of the WEDGE proposal. This important decision not only affirmed his role as "community chaplain" but also provided the congregation with an authentic relationship to its immediate community. Both Nelson and Lincoln were then secure enough to permit each other their separateness. Each was becoming more of the unique person that he alone was. The fact that each was beginning to cultivate a deeper relationship which facilitated the growth of the other was itself a measure of the growth that both had achieved. In spite of the candid comments which characterized their view of each other at the beginning of the project, the center of evaluation and change was unquestionably within themselves. By the end of the project both of them had made the transition from object orientation ("renewal of the church" or "radical social change") to person centeredness ("renewal begins with me").

The personal experience of these two ministers may be described as their gradual acceptance of themselves and each other in the process of becoming. They came to the realization that both were a "fluid process, not a fixed and static entity; a flowing river of change, not a block of solid material; a continually changing constellation of potentialities, not a fixed quantity of traits." [6] Consequently, they stopped using the term "renewal," as if the church had originally been a finished product which needed to be rediscovered in our time. Instead they realized that, like themselves, the church had always been in the process of becoming. Support for this view came from many people who were sharing in the same process of change. Bruce Larson and Ralph Osborne summed it up:

> In both the past and the present, the Church is in a process, moving toward fulfillment of its calling. We have nothing of perfection to which we may return; we have no golden age to which our deepest longings draw up; we have no plumbline from the past which is adequate for the Church of the future. Not *renewal* but *a new thing* is our concern as we begin to witness God's fulfillment of his own word spoken through the prophet Isaiah: 'Remember not the former things, nor consider the things of old. Behold, I am doing a new thing; now it springs forth, do you not perceive it?' (Isaiah 43.18-19). [7]

The "new thing" at Lake Avenue Church did not just happen. It was the result of careful planning on the part of three interrelated organizations—a church, a seminary, and a denominational agency. The representatives of these organizations—a layman, an academic dean, and a denominational executive—were available as a source of support and encouragement to Nelson and Lincoln throughout the project. The way in which a traditional urban church was chosen and then agreed to participate in this experiment shows how God was preparing the way for this "new thing" that was about to spring forth.

[6] Carl R. Rogers, *On Becoming a Person* (Boston: Houghton Mifflin Company, 1961), p. 122.

[7] Bruce Larson and Ralph Osborne, *The Emerging Church* (Waco, Texas: Word, Incorporated, 1970), p. 11.

Having met the two men whose lives were caught up in and drastically changed by the project, it is now possible to examine the process of institutional change more closely. The book is organized around automotive terms in order to highlight the process of change. It is easy to think of the steps that go into designing, testing, and using an automobile. The life span of a good car from the time the idea is originated on the drawing board to the final stage of salvage for useable parts is about fifteen years. The transposition of terminology for institutional change in a church with that of a motor vehicle will accentuate certain aspects of the process.

An examination of the chapter headings will reveal that the five-year experiment is only equivalent to the beginning of an automobile's life span. Our imaginary car moves from the drawing board to the assembly line where transmission trouble is detected. Once in operation the car performs at a record-breaking speed, but the driver soon confronts an unexpected detour and almost has a collision with another vehicle. By yielding right of way he continues his journey until forced to stop for refueling. In the meantime the driver takes time to check the map to be sure that he knows where he will be going when he starts up again. Then he is off again. This kind of cycle will be repeated thousands of times before the vehicle is discarded. Yet each ride presents a new challenge.

The five-year experiment was the beginning of a new challenge for the Lake Avenue Church. It can also provide insight into the kind of unique challenge that confronts your church.

Looking Ahead to Chapter 2

A church that is successful usually has little reason to change. Yet a few people had the vision that a strong church could take an objective look at its reason for existence and respond with a new program which would more adequately fulfill its mission to the world. The setting chosen for this quest was a typical urban environment in an intermediate metropolitan area. The method chosen to implement the vision was experimentation, a trial-and-error approach aimed at testing various options that were open to the congregation. Against the background of an illustrious past, chapter 2 describes the process of "Designing a New Model" for the future ministry of a traditional urban church.

2   Designing a New Model

When preparing a design for a new automobile, it is important to study the trends in previous designs. The changes in style and shape are often striking. It is essential to combine the best features of the past and new ideas which reflect the latest designs.

The beginning of any renewal process in the church is an acknowledgment of the need for balance between *continuity* and *change*. Continuity comes from an appreciation of the heritage which makes each church unique. Change comes from an openness to the horizon which is not yet visible. Designing a new model for Lake Avenue Church meant that its illustrious history would have to be taken seriously. It also presupposed that its future ministry would emerge from the willingness to remain open to changes.

Appreciation for Continuity

Lake Avenue Baptist Church of Rochester, New York, is one of fifty congregations in the American Baptist Convention which has over one thousand members on its roll. Officially known as Lake Avenue Memorial Baptist Church and Society, its leadership in the denomination is due largely to a generous benevolent budget and outstanding preaching. Whereas the majority of the congregation gladly accept the funding responsibility for mission and the personal stimulation of inspired preaching, they actually attend a church on an island in relation to the immediate urban environment. This kind of isolationist position is a fairly recent development in the church's history but was nevertheless inevitable because of the continual dispersion of its members throughout the metropolitan area. In fact, a recent survey in Rochester indicated that Lake Avenue Church has one of the most widely scattered memberships of any Protestant congregation in the city. How could a largely suburban congregation which continues to relate to a centralized meeting place find a handle for community mission? This troubling question undergirded the early phase of the project. An appreciation of this schizophrenic tendency will be enhanced by a brief summary of the church's past history.

Established as a mission of the First Baptist Church of Rochester, New York, in 1866, shortly after the end of the Civil War, "the Memorial Chapel" became a "Regular Baptist Church" with 106 charter members on February 10, 1871. The little chapel was erected on the triangle formed by the intersection of Jones Avenue and Ambrose Street with Lake Avenue. This location at the northern extremity of the city near a cow pasture (later called Jones Park) provided a tranquil setting for its dedication as a memorial to the return of peace after four years of civil strife. Most of the original members lived within a one-mile radius of the church. From its beginning Lake Avenue Baptist Church was primarily known as a prominent supporter of missions; that is, they expressed benevolent concern by giving food, clothes, and money to people at home and abroad. During the pastorate of Dr. Albert W. Beaven (1909-1929), the church sent fifty cents of every dollar raised to some form of missionary work. During this period missionaries who entered full-time vocational Christian service from the Lake Avenue Church could be found in many parts of the world from a Christian center in Ohio to a medical center in India. The church was also instrumental in founding the Hebard Street Italian Mission for the larger number of immigrants coming into the city from 1910 to 1930. Many volunteers were recruited from the church membership for the Americanization effort as well as Sunday school and recreational programs. An expanding membership made it possible to erect a departmentalized educational building and to redesign the sanctuary in 1917 and 1918. The dedication of the new building at the close of World War I added new meaning to the original "Memorial Chapel." This golden age of the church is associated with the charismatic leadership of Dr. Beaven.

The flight to the suburbs started to take its toll on the church membership in the period just prior to World War II. Although Dr. Whitney S. K. Yeaple continued to build upon Dr. Beaven's popularity (the resident membership reached its peak of 2,800 in 1933 during his pastorate 1929-1940), the new trend toward mobility accelerated by the automobile allowed more and more people to move away from the changing neighborhood of the church. When Dr. Gerald Watkins became the church's pastor in 1941, the resident membership had declined to 1,821. Dr. George W. Hill, who became pastor in 1954, started with 1,738 resident members. With a budget of $100,000, the persistent interest in missionary work was maintained at a level of thirty-five cents from every dollar. In spite of the continuing trend of membership decline, few churches anywhere could be described as being more successful in terms of pastoral care and organizational efficiency. The coming of the Rev. W. Herbert Grant as minister of Christian education in 1955 added strength to an educational ministry which was already well respected for its innovative and experimental leadership in the field. The Rev. Charles A. Thunn became the associate minister in 1959 with a major responsibility for pastoral visitation. The continuing dispersion of the church membership left less than 1 percent of the congregation residing in the immediate neighborhood (one-mile radius around the church) at that time.

The gulf between the church and its community was evident in 1954 when a thirteen-year-old neighborhood resident dropped out of church school. From her present involvement as a prominent community leader, Mrs. Jenette Valdez describes Lake Avenue Church as she remembers it from a local teenager's perspective:

Who knows, maybe Lake Avenue Baptist Church has always stood on the same triangular parcel of land between Jones Avenue and Ambrose Street. Looks about the same as it did eighteen years ago when I stopped attending—big, firm, and silent. Seems peculiar how it was about the same time the church was surveying the needs of *its community* that I received a Bible for some attendance award, and then I left. Looking back over the years, I think Lake Avenue Baptist Church and most other churches, I guess, wrongly emphasized a one-sided view of Jesus. I don't believe he would have made much of an impact on many people if he just stood there with outstretched arms saying: "Come!" Funny how the same church taught me to think of him as one who moved among crowds and went where there was need. After a while, the Sunday greeting of the ushers standing inside the doors seemed awfully routine. They would bid me welcome and farewell. One day I left and wasn't even missed when I came no more.

It is ironical that a neighborhood teenager quietly faded away at the same time a few young adults, who were related to the church's Sunday Night Club, began to grasp a new urban image for the congregation. In the summer of 1955 they attended the Recreation Lab at the American Baptist Assembly in Green Lake, Wisconsin, where they learned about the Juvenile Protection Program of the American Baptist Home Mission Societies. Upon their return to Rochester, the dream of developing a community center for neighborhood children at the church soon became a reality. Necessary leadership for the center was provided by a student minister who was assigned to the church by the Colgate Rochester Divinity School in the fall of 1955. While living in the neighborhood, he and his wife Cynthia recruited lay leadership from the Sunday Night Club which sponsored the Community Center. New interest in the local community led the church to request the denominational Juvenile Protection Program to conduct a church and community survey which was completed by Lawrence Janssen and Nick Neufeld in February, 1955. The coming of another student minister in the fall of 1960 provided continuity of leadership for the Community Center. Because he also lived in the neighborhood, a bridge of understanding between the church and its community continued to be built.

In addition to Dr. Hill's preparing a climate for change through his regular pulpit ministry on Sunday morning, further impetus was gained from a preaching mission in 1962 led by President Gene Bartlett of the Colgate Rochester Divinity School. The immediate effect of these special services was the formation of two Bible study groups which consisted of younger progressive members of the congregation. These ten couples quickly realized that their small groups were the most meaningful part of their relationship to the church. The convenor of one Bible study group became chairman of the Christian social concern committee, which joined forces with the building council in making another study of the immediate neighborhood. Their joint recommendation was that the church should remain at its present location and renovate its facilities for an expanded community ministry. The commitment of the congregation to this decision on January 9, 1963, involved an expenditure of $370,000, a vital step in setting the stage for the experiment. Throughout this renovation program Dr. Hill lifted the sights of the congregation beyond "paint, plaster, and plumbing" to the need for better facilities to implement the church's mission.

At the same time the Christian social concern committee was dissolved in favor of a board of social action. An annually elected committee was replaced by a continuous board made up of rotating three-year memberships. This shift in priority gave the church's urban mission in Rochester an equal status alongside the traditional boards of (world) missions, Christian education, deacons, deaconesses, and trustees. Dr. Hill and the chairman of this board of social action discussed with the Home Mission Societies and the Divinity School ways in which the Lake Avenue Church could more effectively minister to a changing urban community. In the fall of 1963 a school of missions dealing with "The Changing City Challenges the Church" added a sense of urgency to the need for an expanded community ministry. The time was right for the church to take another important step in its history.

Acceptance of Change

A convergence of concern from key representatives of the church, a theological seminary, and a denominational agency led to the development of a five-year experimental project in church renewal. Ray Kicklighter, a research physicist with the Eastman Kodak Company, embodied the kind of lay leadership which was at the heart of the quest for renewal at the Lake Avenue Church. Dean Milton C. Froyd of the Divinity School (later named Provost of Colgate Rochester Divinity School/Bexley Hall) was aware of the large number of seminarians who no longer considered the institutional church as an option for the Christian ministry. Dr. Harvey A. Everett of the American Baptist Home Mission Societies had a comprehensive understanding about the problems which were confronted in inner-city ministry from his broad experience throughout the American Baptist Convention. In 1964 the three cooperating institutions proposed that an urban experiment in church renewal should be centered at the Lake Avenue Church, for a minimum of five years.

Although the ground rules were defined rather loosely to provide maximum freedom for experimentation, several common concerns emerged in the early stages of joint planning for the project: (1) The choice of the Lake Avenue Church meant that this experiment would be conducted in an older, well-established congregation which was operating from a position of strength. The Home Mission Societies had considerable doubt about the validity of using mission funds to prolong the life of dying congregations in the inner city. In many instances the basic decisions about the direction of their ministry had not been faced soon enough to make a difference either in their approach to mission or in their continuing survival. It was decided that it might be easier to determine the basic steps that go into a change of direction "from tradition to mission" by starting with a well-established church. (2) This experiment would be conducted in Rochester, an intermediate metropolitan area with a population of 500,000 in which the magnitude of urban problems should be somewhat manageable. The overwhelming complexity of ministry in the major cities of our nation left many church leaders bewildered. It was felt that a handle for renewal could be found more naturally where the forces of urban change could be identified more clearly. (3) This project would depend heavily upon the resources of an unusually gifted group of lay persons at the Lake Avenue Church. Although the leadership of the clergy was not ignored, it was felt from the beginning that the key to the experiment would be in the hands of the laity. As the key spokesman for the church's laity, Ray Kicklighter expressed two basic assumptions about the experiment in interpreting the new venture to the congregation: "The major activities of the Protestant church are out of touch with the lives of people in a large area of urban society, and the church is renewable."

The three cooperating institutions decided that the availability of an additional minister on the staff of the church would give the project a visible focus. This person would be free from the traditional preaching, administrative, educational, and pastoral duties in order to concentrate on developing a strategy for renewal. He would also work with a select number of seminarians in specialized training for urban ministry. On January 8, 1964, the congregation voted to participate in a five-year experimental ministry with the Home Mission Societies and the Divinity School for the purpose of exploring the shape of church renewal in a typical urban setting. Ray Kicklighter's analogy of research and development projects in industry helped the church become more at ease about the experimental nature of the new venture. Later he became chairman of the ministerial selection committee which sought staff leadership for the project. Although he was more comfortable in the role of long-range renewal strategist, he also felt a personal responsibility to direct the Community Center until a full-time staff person could be found. His theoretical prodding and practical involvement exemplified the admonition of a respected church leader that "the first duty of the layman in his local church is to be a nuisance."

There was a lingering impression that renewal in this particular situation would start by doing something more about ministering to the immediate neighborhood around the church. The ministerial selection committee had the task of finding a staff person who was not only familiar with the urban challenge but who also had the kind of academic background which would be respected by divinity school students. The way in which the committee entered into conversation with William R. Nelson reflects a mutual quest for direction while looking "through a glass darkly."

The insistence of the committee upon a strong identification with the neighborhood caused them to ask the Nelson family to live near the church, a precedent which several student ministers had already established. This urban orientation of the position forced Nelson to make a basic decision about the direction of his ministry. The conflict between graduate study at the Princeton Theological Seminary and an inner-city congregation in Trenton, New Jersey, had been dividing his energies for several years. A partial choice was made by remaining at the Clinton Avenue Baptist Church after receiving the Doctor of Theology degree in 1963. The desire to get specialized training in urban ministry had led him to several urban workshops sponsored by the Home Mission Societies and finally to the Urban Training Center for Christian Mission in Chicago. Yet it became increasingly difficult to live with academic aspirations in the midst of a difficult urban parish.

The initial conversations in Rochester seemed to be fruitless when Nelson refused to cut his long-standing tie with the academic community. At first, this academic rope seemed like the only security which would keep him from falling into the unknown abyss of the urban challenge. His fear of the unknown was disguised by a fervent plea to shift the "anchor" of the project from the church to the seminary. Considering the number of years that he had spent in advanced New Testament studies, Nelson was interested in protecting his academic investment. Although he had already been functioning effectively in a complex urban setting, it was extremely difficult for him to cut the rope and give up the dream of a more formal academic career. Dean Froyd responded eloquently to this dilemma in a lengthy and persuasive letter to William R. Nelson on March 17, 1965. This letter became the springboard for the experimental project:

> For more than a decade we have been unloading the big guns of our biblical and theological insights upon the nature and purpose of the church in the modern world, and yet for all our talk about the need for renewal we still find precious few places where such renewal actually takes on concrete and visible form. From the outset two things became clear in this quest: first, the primary object of our concern was the church and its possibility for renewal; second, the object of this concern had to be viewed not in terms of the church in general but the church in some specific, identifiable place. While, from the standpoint of the Home Mission Societies and the Divinity School, the training of ministers was of immediate concern, neither body was under any illusion as to what had to take prior claim—the issue of the renewal of the church itself. Out of this conviction emerged conversations with a number of churches which eventually led to a decision to work with the Lake Avenue Baptist Church.
>
> Central to the task before us is the need for providing for another minister on the staff of the Lake Avenue Baptist Church whose primary task will be to work with the ministers and the entire congregation at the point of the rediscovery of the church as a people of God and its mission in the world. Because an inescapable part of that mission, and perhaps the most difficult part, is to be seen in its witness in the city and immediate community, this becomes a major, but by no means exclusive, point of thrust. When we refer to the term "teaching minister," we actually have in mind something with which you would be familiar in your Old Testament studies. We are thinking here of the teacher, not as the traditional pedagogue, but as one who saw the teaching task in a way that identified word with deed in ministry. You may recall the reference in the Creation story to the Hebrew word *dubahr*, "and God said." The word conveys an identification of saying with doing, the word spoken with the visible consequences of that which was said— this is something of what we have in mind when we speak of the role of the teaching minister. It is this concept that is not very common in the teaching procedure which governs the life of the church.

The point of no return, therefore, was accepting the requirement to live in the midst of the urban challenge, rather than speculating about it from an ivy-covered tower. Since the entire family was involved in the consequences of this decision, William and his wife Colleen wondered about the influence of this kind of environment upon their two preschool children. Another attractive job offer in higher education made their decision even more difficult. At that point a basic conviction about God's call for direct involvement in urban ministry took precedence. It soon became apparent that the greater the risk, the greater would be the possibilities for personal enrichment and Christian growth.

What was the urban environment to which the Nelsons were committing themselves and their children? It was a working-class neighborhood inhabited largely by first and second generation Italian families. The predominant influence of Roman Catholicism was symbolized by an old-line Italian parish, St. Anthony of Padua, and by a former Irish parish, St. Patrick's church. The Nelsons bought and renovated a one-family house on Ambrose Street in August, 1965. In addition to being midway between the two Roman Catholic churches, their new home was also within sight of Lake Avenue Church. For the first time in recent years the church had a full-time staff person in its immediate neighborhood. Two of the other full-time ministers lived in the suburbs, and a third lived in the outer fringe of the city.

In September, 1965, the experiment was officially inaugurated when Nelson assumed the new position of teaching minister on the church's staff. It was understood from the start that the one chosen to lead the church in this venture would also become an experiment himself. His personal involvement had been assured by the requirement of living in the immediate neighborhood of the church and also by the additional request that his biblical studies and sociological awareness be supplemented by a quarter of clinical pastoral education. From the perspective of the ministerial selection committee the latter exposure to the discipline of psychology was viewed as a safeguard against certain egocentric tendencies which were evident in the preliminary conversations.

The urban training dimension of the project brought on the scene William F. Lincoln, a middler at the Colgate Rochester Divinity School, who had a strong interest in social work. In two years of identifying with welfare recipients who lived in a deteriorating neighborhood near the church, Lincoln created for himself the position of "community chaplain" in Brown Square. His effectiveness was recognized by the Home Mission Societies so that additional funds were provided to extend his two-year training program for two more years as an advanced urban intern. By finding full-time secular employment for the fifth year, continuity was maintained with the five-year experiment. His hesitancy to move on until the right kind of church-related position opened up enabled him to maintain his quasi-staff relationship at the Lake Avenue Church beyond the five-year experiment.

The staff of a chemistry lab in an industrial firm gathered one morning to meet their new supervisor. He was introduced to the group and set everyone at ease by saying: "No one in this lab will be doing adequate research unless at least 50 percent of his experiments are not satisfactory." He realized that something could be learned from experiments which do not prove successful as well as those which do. Because of the conviction that dedication to scientific truth is more important than a determination to succeed, he provided an environment in which members of his research group were free to fail. This spirit of experimentation enabled a traditional urban church to build upon its past strength and to project a design for its future potential.

Looking Ahead to Chapter 3

The initial focus for experimentation was the immediate community in which the church was located. Rather than try to serve all the world, a serious attempt was made to relate more personally to the specific people who lived within a one-half-mile radius of the church building. The time and energy which went into getting acquainted with this neighborhood was necessary in order to shift gears from *giving to missions* to *involvement in mission*. Indisputable evidence of the "new thing" that God was doing took the form of rediscovering mission at the local level. Chapter 3 describes the community involvement which resulted in overcoming the "Transmission Trouble" which in recent years had limited the church's mission within its immediate community to a faithful few.

3   Overcoming Transmission Trouble

The enormous step from the drawing board to the assembly line is necessary if the production process is to result in a new automobile. However, this difference is often obscured in ecclesiastical circles. Most churches have become mesmerized into thinking that talking about mission is doing it. This exercise in self-deception has become a science with many liberal-minded churchmen who have settled for giving their money and talking about giving themselves. More traditional churchmen tend to admit openly that the contrast between Christian principle and Christian practice leaves much to be desired. In either case the actual movement from word to deed requires a certain amount of trial and error which is characterized by the freedom to fail.

On an automotive assembly line the basic design is tested for performance by means of a rigorous inspection system which includes all the necessary readjustments. One of the most important mechanisms is the transmission, the gears by which power is transmitted from the engine to the axle which propels the vehicle. In addition to many optional features which it may have, the transmission must function properly if the vehicle is to move at all.

Because the design for the new model at the Lake Avenue Church put a spotlight on the church's changing community, it was not too much of a surprise that the basic difficulty was found to be transmission trouble. It had become increasingly difficult for the suburban-oriented church members to relate to a working-class community with which they had almost nothing in common. One observer said quite frankly: "The beginning of a new urban approach to church renewal for the Lake Avenue Church can be traced to a rock that a neighborhood youth threw through a beautiful stained-glass window." This incident which happened about 1955 merely dramatized the gap which had gradually developed between the church and its immediate community. Although admittedly a minor incident which was soon forgotten, this act of vandalism was a symptom of more complex transmission trouble which made it extremely difficult to minister to a changing community in which the church members no longer lived.

In addition to its mechanical meaning, the term "transmission" also has the theological connotation of passing the Christian faith on to one's successors (cf. 1 Corinthians 11:23a). The situation was further complicated because the majority of neighborhood residents were Roman Catholics. Any serious attempts to work with neighborhood residents could be interpreted as proselytizing. The complexities of urban change had gradually immobilized the congregation to the extent that some dramatic new thrust was needed to overcome this inertia.

There was an acknowledgment from the beginning of the experiment that renewal would be closely associated with community ministry. This view was highlighted by entitling the enlarged staff and program budget associated with the project "Our Mission to the Community." Funds from the Home Mission Societies were matched by the church in a total annual budget of $19,000. The close tie with the Divinity School was reflected by their assigning two students for specialized urban training. The possibility of feedback to the seminary was assured by naming Nelson a "Lecturer in Field Education."

The first six months of the project were a period of moratorium in which existing programs were maintained as inherited. In addition to getting acquainted with the resources of the metropolitan area and the history of the particular church to which he was related, Nelson also needed time to find his place on the church staff and on the newly created board of social action. As a member of the staff team, he was directly responsible to the senior minister, Dr. George W. Hill, the same line of accountability which was already established with respect to the associate minister and the director of Christian education. A part-time choir director-organist and two regular student ministers had been related to the staff for many years. Nelson had under his supervision two additional students, William F. Lincoln and Patrick E. Murphy, who met weekly during the first year in a tutorial seminar. A broad-based advisory committee was available to Nelson as an informal source of support during the first two years of the experiment. In addition to Harvey Everett, Milton Froyd, and Ray Kicklighter, the committee also consisted of Rev. Harrison Williams, executive minister of the Monroe Baptist Association and Rev. Herbert D. White, executive director of the board for urban ministry, Rochester Area Council of Churches.

Moratorium for Research

The lack of any expectation about producing instantaneous new programs helped to minimize Nelson's initial anxieties. He was free to examine the transmission trouble which caused the church to be at a temporary standstill with respect to community ministry. One of the most helpful keys for becoming acquainted with the neighborhood was learning the many ways in which it could be described. Converging insights tended to reinforce one another by comparing census tracts, public school zones, and city planning areas.

Census tracts provided some basic statistics which had already been unearthed in previous surveys made by the congregation. Within a one-mile radius of the church, there was a general downgrading of housing conditions. Over 50 percent of the structures were built prior to 1899. According to the 1960 census, 10 percent of the 10,521 dwelling units in the area were deteriorating and 3 percent were dilapidated. Although the area is predominantly Italian, the immigration of Negroes and Puerto Ricans increased from 14 in 1950 to 275 in 1960. A total population decline of 9 percent between 1950 and 1960 pointed to the growing tendency to abandon the crowded conditions of the city for the more open spaces of suburbia.

The public school zones provided another key for studying the community. The school enrollment figures confirmed the impression that the area was heavily populated by young married couples with small children. The racial mixture in the schools also showed a gradual increase of Negro and Puerto Rican immigration into the area. The nonwhite enrollment of Elementary School #5 in one of the most rapidly deteriorating sections was up to 32 percent in 1965. However, this percentage was not truly characteristic of the community because many children came from other parts of the city to attend special education classes there.

The City Planning Commission provided still a different way of viewing the neighborhood. The northwest sector of Rochester consists of two planning communities: LYELL to the south and KODAK to the north. The immediate neighborhood of the Lake Avenue Church is the eastern part of the LYELL planning community which stretches along the Genesee River from the Inner Loop to Driving Park Avenue as shown on the map on page 15. This eastern part of the LYELL planning community is called the Edgerton Area. This area is in turn divided into three planning areas (BROWN SQUARE, EDGERTON PARK, and OTIS) which provide the framework for a more detailed description of the neighborhood.

The point of the triangular slice at the lower part of the northwest sector is the planning area called "Brown Square." This so-called "poverty pocket," or lower-class neighborhood, is bounded by Allen Street (Inner Loop), the former Erie Canal, Lyell Avenue, and the Genesee River. St. Patrick's Church stands like a fortress in the shadow of the Kodak tower, as if the massive phallic symbol which dominates the neighborhood needed the protective care of mother church. Elementary School #5 is a few blocks away. Because this southern extremity of the northwest sector is a declining residential fringe ("inner city") bordering on the city's central business district, a large number of welfare tenants have settled there in marginal housing which is largely owned by absentee landlords. The transient white, black, and Spanish-speaking newcomers have little in common with the more permanent Italian property owners. The name "Brown Square" comes from the second oldest public playground in the country, which occupies a square city block in the center of the neighborhood. Its continuous recreational use through the years was interrupted only periodically to host such gala attractions as the Ringling Brothers, Barnum and Bailey Circus.

The elongated working-class neighborhood along the west bank of the Genesee River is the planning area known as "Edgerton Park." The area bounded by Lyell Avenue, the former Erie Canal, and Driving Park Avenue gets the name "Edgerton Park" from the large public playground in the middle of the neighborhood which provides extensive open space for Jefferson High School. The predominant Italian ethnic group looks disparagingly upon blacks who are moving into the upper part of the area, especially in multiple dwellings on Fulton Avenue and tenements on Lake Avenue. The architectural elegance of Lake Avenue Church and

St. Anthony's Church provides a strong stabilizing influence upon the neighborhood since both churches have recently spent large sums of money improving their facilities. Another positive influence in the area is Christ Presbyterian Church, which is in the process of becoming a neighborhood congregation. Grace Methodist Church and Holy Rosary Church are interested primarily in the Maplewood planning area north of Driving Park Avenue in the Kodak community where most of their members lived.

The smaller triangle west of the former Erie Canal is the Otis planning area, which is also bounded by Lyell Avenue and Burrows Street. The visible evidence of deterioration is most obvious on Murray Street, which is midway between the Lyell Avenue Baptist and Holy Apostles churches. A bitter dispute over bussing black children into an Otis elementary school had left many emotional scars on the residents of this lower-middle-class neighborhood.

This multifaceted way of viewing the church's immediate neighborhood grew out of contact with many key agencies in the city. As a result of Nelson's teaming up with a newly arrived Presbyterian community minister, Rev. James Rice, a working relationship was established with governmental, educational, and social agencies. The freedom that both men had from traditional church assignments made it possible for them to conduct their own urban seminar with key decision makers on the urban scene. At the same time they compared insights gained from their previous urban experience in Trenton and Chicago.

Rice's involvement in Chicago provided an added resource during the early stages of ecumenical planning for community ministry. As pastor of Christ Presbyterian Church in the heart of Lincoln Park for the previous eight years, he had been a leader in the development of the Northside Cooperative Ministry, one of the few working models of interfaith cooperation at the time. Twenty-two congregations, including two suburban churches, cooperatively sponsored a young adult ministry through a coffee-house and bookstore called "The Door." In addition to other age-group ministries, task forces also formed to deal with metropolitan issues.

The initial period of exploration which Nelson and Rice spent in accumulating resources for social service and social change provided a backdrop for viewing their respective sectors of the city. The highly organized southwest sector where Rice was working provided a sharp contrast to the almost totally unorganized northwest sector with which Nelson was getting acquainted. Although the early phase of the experimental project seemed slow in getting started, the systematic study of community resources pointed the way beyond the transmission trouble which had caused the church to feel helpless in the midst of overwhelming pressures of urban change.

The initial impression of those involved in planning the experiment was that the church had a strong internal ministry among its members. The missing link seemed to be the development of more specific opportunities for service in the local community. The strong issue-oriented preaching ministry of Dr. Hill had set the climate for social action. Rather than leaving people frustrated with guilt feelings because of what they were not doing, it was hoped that the expansion of community projects in the neighborhood would provide the setting for expressing Christian faith in action. Therefore, one approach to overcoming the transmission trouble was the need to make general challenges from the pulpit operational in the lives of specific individuals in the congregation.

Since the Nelson family lived on Ambrose Street, their close identification with the immediate community provided the church with a natural opening into the lives of their Italian neighbors. Like most members of the Lake Avenue Church, the Nelsons exhibited a non-apologetic middle-class style of living from the start by using the whole house for their family. The norm for this working-class community was for the homeowner to live downstairs and to rent out one or more apartments in the rest of the house.

While the extensive renovation of their one-family house was consistent with the Nelson's accustomed standard of living, the financial impracticality of upgrading the property became painfully apparent five years later when the sale of the house was subjected to the neighborhood real estate standards. From the perspective of a "post factum sociological interpretation," Nelson had been asked to enter into a five-year experiment of "participation observation." [1] Keeping in touch with area residents had become in-

---

[1] Herbert J. Gans, *The Urban Villagers* (New York: The Free Press, 1962). A study of group and class life of Italian-Americans (especially pp. 336-350) describes a social scientist's experience of living among Italian-Americans in the West End of Boston. His study provided some basic guidelines for understanding a similar environment in Rochester.

creasingly difficult for both the suburban-oriented members and professional staff of the church because they were looked upon as weekend intruders or at best visitors. The majority of the older church members had become upward mobiles whose improved economic status permitted them to live in better neighborhoods. Most of the newer members were commuting to the church from the fringes of the city or the suburbs. The main outlet for the few members who felt a specific responsibility for ministering to the people in the neighborhood area of the church was the Community Center.

Although there was some degree of impatience in working with neighborhood children who had little influence in the realm of social change, the need for the community center program sponsored by the church during the previous ten years was quickly reaffirmed. The primary social unit in the area is the extended family and close relatives living nearby. Membership in this adult-oriented peer-group society is based primarily on kinship except for godparents who, because of their closeness, are given quasi-familial status. Children are expected to adapt to the rules of the adult-centered home. It did not take the Nelsons long to realize that their own middle-class values were reflected in a child-centered family pattern in which their personal wishes were often deferred in order to give special consideration to the social needs of their two small children. This same orientation was characteristic of most of the adult staff of the Community Center, who found it quite natural to respond to the recreational, artistic, and interpersonal needs of neighborhood children. The special interest which the volunteer lay staff extended to the children was an appreciated contrast to the street rules of their own peer-group society. Since the majority of the children coming to the center were from Italian Catholic families related to St. Anthony's parish, it was understood from the beginning of the community center program that there would be no religious instruction of any kind for them at a Protestant church.

During the 1965–1966 school year the Community Center continued to attract about one hundred neighborhood children from kindergarten through sixth grade every Saturday morning at the Lake Avenue Church. A lay staff of twelve persons provided recreational and craft activities for the children in four smaller groups. The only significant change in the program during this year was the introduction of 4-H materials which added considerable sophistication to the craft activities. When Lincoln became impatient with the limitations of a child-oriented program in the middle of the first year, the other urban trainee from the Divinity School continued to oversee the program by himself. Pat Murphy realized that it was helpful to have some organized contact with the immediate neighborhood while new routes for community ministry were being explored. As important as it was to work with neighborhood children, it was generally recognized that the church's transmission trouble could only be overcome by responding to the concerns of neighborhood youth and adults.

Clergymen as Change Agents

A growing number of concerned persons at Lake Avenue Church expressed interest in serving the church's changing community. Yet it was during an inadvertent street-corner conversation between Nelson and a Roman Catholic priest that the transmission clicked into gear and started moving the church on a new route. Nelson's presence on Ambrose Street was not only a natural way of getting to know area residents, but it also placed him in a common parish with neighborhood clergy. The spontaneous encounter between a Protestant minister and a Catholic priest took place on Ambrose Street midway between Nelson's home and the Lake Avenue Church. On this neutral ground which was symbolically in the midst of their common parish, the cautious relations between Protestants and Catholics in the neighborhood started to change.

Father Paul Freemesser, an assistant pastor at St. Anthony's Church, was a jovial, young priest who took a special interest in the youth of his parish. He was also open to the new ecumenical mood of the post-Vatican II era. Before leaving the street corner, Nelson and Freemesser decided to bring two more local clerics into their newly discovered interfaith fellowship. Nelson made contact with the Rev. Robert Booher, pastor of Christ Presbyterian Church, and Freemesser spoke to Father James Russell, the new assistant pastor at St. Anthony's Church. About a week later these four men arranged to meet together for the first time. Father Russell brought with him several members of the Legion of Mary, a Catholic lay society dedicated to assisting the clergy with parish visitation. Although ecumenical discussions like "Living Room

Dialogues" had been officially approved by the Vatican Council, there were few examples of this form of cross-fertilization in Rochester during the fall of 1965. The informal get-together of representatives from three Edgerton Area churches seemed to indicate that much could be gained through sharing each other's interests and concerns.

Admittedly there was very little thought about a self-conscious ecumenical strategy during the early months of getting acquainted. Gradually a plan started taking shape. The first gear of the new acceleration into community ministry was the determination to activate the dormant Northwest Clergy Association. Although the original nucleus of two Protestant ministers and two Catholic priests sparked this development, a similar desire for more dialogue and better understanding was also expressed by their colleagues. Over a dozen interested clergymen started meeting every other week in order to learn more about their common parish. A variety of resource persons were invited to give a descriptive picture of the northwest part of the city. Similarly, Jim Rice related his experience with the Northside Cooperative Ministry in Chicago. Several months of discussion led to the general conclusion that community ministry could be developed more effectively together than separately.

The second gear was the emergence of an action-reflection group at the Lake Avenue Church. A leading spokesman for the Italian-American community around Jones Park was invited to speak to this core group of lay persons from the Lake Avenue Church who were interested in community ministry. In addition to being a lifetime resident of the neighborhood, he was also a lawyer, a Republican ward leader, and a trustee of St. Anthony's Church. This small group of fifteen persons from Lake Avenue Church was the "fallout" from a School of Missions dealing with the challenge of the city. Since the Lake Avenue Church laity did not live in the city, it was decided to explore the neighborhood interest in developing an ongoing community organization with a similar group of Roman Catholic residents from St. Anthony's Church. A combined meeting was scheduled to take place in the new building of St. Anthony's Church, which was valued at over a million dollars. News of this development spread to the newly activated Northwest Clergy Association. Four other neighborhood churches decided to send representatives to the meeting.

The third gear was the consensus that the greatest need in the area was to enable the residents to form a local community organization. On January 9, 1966, everyone was surprised to find St. Anthony's Church Hall filled with more than one hundred persons for the constituting assembly of the Edgerton Area Neighborhood Association (E.A.N.A.). In order to present an interfaith, nonpartisan plea for a local community organization, brief speeches were made by Booher and Freemesser as well as Republican and Democratic ward leaders. There was a general consensus that the time was right to develop a community action group for the neighborhood. The base of support seemed broad enough at that point to get started. Temporary officers were elected immediately. Their first assignment was to form various committees related to community needs and to begin mobilizing community residents. No one seemed to notice that the majority of interest in the new organization came from property owners who had a vested interest in protecting their neighborhood from the infringement of "undesirables." This term was freely used to signify black and Spanish-speaking people in general or welfare recipients and tenants in particular. It was also not apparent at the time that St. Anthony's Church had a citywide reputation as a front organization for the local Republican political machine.

On that same night another significant development took place which few people noticed. A Trinitarian nun, Sister Rose Vincent from St. Patrick's Church, appeared on the scene. Although living at a Cenacle in the 1964 riot-stricken Third Ward, she commuted daily by car to Brown Square in order to conduct "released-time" religious education classes for the children of her assigned parish. Father Freemesser prefaced his remarks to the constituting assembly with the announcement of his imminent transfer to another parish in the city. Sister Rose would soon fill the chair which he vacated in the nuclear interfaith fellowship as a representative of St. Patrick's Church.

The high level of interest at the initial organizational meeting of E.A.N.A. was followed by the drafting and approval of a constitution. The four-member constitution and bylaws committee which Nelson chaired was a microcosm of the total organization. It consisted of a Protestant minister, a Roman Catholic lay person, a Republican ward supervisor, and a Democratic ward chairman. The purposes of the neighborhood association were oriented around six basic needs of the community which became the task-orientation for working committees on zoning, housing, land use, public safety, recreation, and education. Yet a key issue was needed in order to focus the concern of the organization. The earlier unsuccessful fight with "junkyard" establishments in the Brown Square area was revived by the new Neighborhood Association. The high piles of scrap and bad odors from open burning were obvious violations of city codes. Several area meetings were held to dramatize the problem before city officials. Picket lines in front of the main scrapyard offender received prompt radio and TV coverage.

Although the march was supposedly sponsored by three Neighborhood Associations, the majority of participants were housewives from the neighboring community on the west side of the subway bed which formed the rear boundary of the scrapyards. No one seemed to express concern that not a single resident of Brown Square (where the junkyards were located) was present for the march. Nelson participated in the march along with the others as a genuine expression of concern about the health hazard of such an operation in a high-density neighborhood.

A similar march down the subway bed was made by concerned laity from the Lake Avenue Church on Palm Sunday. Photographs of filth and debris along the subway bed which were taken on this march managed to get into the hands of prominent city officials. The next step was to get a representative group from three Neighborhood Associations to attend a meeting of the city council. Protest speeches were made before the council by this coalition of civic groups who shared the concern of E.A.N.A. about code violations. Eventually the Democratic majority on City Council passed a new scrapyard ordinance. Although some neighborhood residents wanted the junkyards removed altogether, the new ordinance at least removed the worst offenses. After a year's struggle, the successful resolution of this issue was interpreted by E.A.N.A. as at least a partial victory.

Some observers felt that it was more than coincidental that this junkyard issue was resolved just in time for the temporary chairman of E.A.N.A. to announce his candidacy for City Council. Of course, this open political affiliation led to his immediate resignation as temporary chairman. Then Mr. Booher reinforced the original church sponsorship of the organization by becoming its duly elected president in the absence of other interested neighborhood leadership. Christ Presbyterian Church had already revised his job description so that the majority of his time could be spent in direct involvement with the neighborhood. An associate minister was called to cover the more traditional pastoral concerns. The fact that the community organization survived this transition period can be attributed only to the personal magnetism and unrelenting persistence of the new president.

Whereas Christ Presbyterian Church channeled some of its most capable leaders into this aspect of community ministry, key members from Lake Avenue Church began to shift their interest to the more needy residents of Brown Square. These "undesirables" did not seem to fit into the protectionist tendencies of property owners who dominated E.A.N.A. At the same time that Nelson had been active on the steering committee of E.A.N.A., Lincoln had been working with tenants and welfare recipients in the Brown Square area. The strain between these two men who differed in their "bureaucratic" and "grass root" approaches to community action was also reflected in the strain between the Edgerton Park and Brown Square communities. In fact, the gnawing persistence of Lincoln about the lack of an authentic voice for the poor in E.A.N.A. caused Nelson to reevaluate the entire process.

In retrospect it seemed that an unlikely coalition of ecumenical churchmanship and partisan politics had tried to force object-oriented goals upon a person-centered community. Nelson perceived that the sociological contrast was between the middle-class behavior of aggressive clergymen and aspiring politicians on the one hand and the working-class behavior of passive, apathetic residents on the other hand. Instead of getting excited about the object-oriented goal of forcing the city to adopt a scrapyard ordinance, most neighborhood residents were more concerned about the person-centered goal of contributing to the solidarity of their peer-group society. This contrast is highlighted in the provocative study of Italian Americans by Herbert J. Gans:

> The object-oriented people will join a group in order to achieve a common purpose; the person-centered ones need the group to become individuals. Consequently, when a set of person-oriented people must act together, they lose interest; they become "selfish," that is, concerned about what common action will do to them as individuals.[2]

[2] Herbert J. Gans, *ibid.,* pp. 90-91.

Perhaps this basic difference lies behind the tendency of middle-class people to view the working class as apathetic about social change. The unconscious existence of this conflict of interest explains the previously mentioned vacuum which gave the northwest sector the reputation for being the least organized part of the city.

Living in the midst of this kind of ambivalence helped Nelson to influence some residents in favor of his object-oriented goals and to be influenced by those who invited him to share their person-centered goals. His inner struggle between organizing programs and responding to people could not be ignored. Nevertheless the presence of a minister from the Lake Avenue Church in the immediate community had provided the extra incentive for overcoming the long standing distance between local Protestants and Catholics. The unlikely coalition of mutual self-interest between a few clergymen and a key politician had resulted in the development of a new structure for mission to the community. The Protestant and Catholic churches had found each other by attempting to respond to the needs of their common parish. E.A.N.A. became the initial bond which brought them together.

A bulletin board in the basement of the Lake Avenue Church contained an unusual picture of a storm on the high seas. It was entitled "wave makers" and described the role of a change agent in the corporate structure of an industrial firm. This obscure display may not have been seen by many people, but it accurately reflected the way in which Nelson interpreted his role in both the church and its immediate community. As a minister on the staff of the church and a resident of the neighborhood, he had provided a rallying point for a core group of restless lay persons who shared his vision of an ecumenical style of community ministry. The careful planning for two years on the design for the project as well as the year of research and testing had paid off. The new design was ready to move out to the main highway and explore the unprecedented route of ecumenical community ministry.

Looking Ahead to Chapter 4

The new route of rediscovering mission at the local level had put the Lake Avenue Church on a course which broke through traditional interdenominational and interfaith barriers. A new spirit of Christian community had emerged from cooperatively confronting neighborhood issues and had led to the development of new ecumenical ministries. The new programs tended to replace existing in-church activities rather than merely contributing to an outside group such as the Neighborhood Association. Experimentation with six new ecumenical programs took place almost simultaneously. Chapter 4 describes the record-breaking speed with which the original organizational development was complemented by programs aimed at personal growth. This initial movement from action to reflection was not an end in itself but a means of pointing the way to an additional avenue for experimentation: the forgotten poor of Brown Square who did not respond to traditional church programs even with a new ecumenical label.

4   Record-Breaking Speed

The thrill of a new car is experienced for the first time when it is taken out on the highway and "opened up." The painstaking attention to the details of design and testing are apparent when the car attains high speed. The exhilaration and freedom of this kind of fulfillment is a reward in itself.

The same feeling of exuberance came from the unexpected rapidity with which the new ecumenical approach to community ministry emerged during the second and third year of the project. The "new thing" that God was doing broke through many of the long-standing barriers that had traditionally separated Protestants and Catholics. What had started as a unilateral ministry with children sponsored by the Lake Avenue Church soon became a multilateral ministry with children, youth, and adults sponsored by most of the churches in the entire northwest sector of the city.

At the same time that the action-oriented goals of E.A.N.A. were being developed, there was also a growing concern for personal growth goals within the nuclear interfaith community. During the course of this organizational development process, a meaningful relationship between four persons was being cultivated. They became the informal planning committee for a maze of new ecumenical programs. The permissive attitude of the Roman Catholic Diocese toward the progressive mood of the post-Vatican II era provided an ideal environment for experimentation. The representatives of four neighboring churches provided the strategy.

Nelson found his niche in the area of organizing programs in response to the common concern of the group. One observer referred to him as "a conceptualizing administrator who can quickly theorize a programmatic response to an articulated need." Booher emerged as the key activist in the group who had a gift for getting programs implemented. He was referred to as "a community organizer with a clerical collar." Father Russell turned out to be the theologian in the group. He had a gift for summarizing the thinking of each person on the basis of the many things that were shared in common, especially the centrality of Jesus Christ. Sister Rose brought a persuasive new influence into the informal core group with her insistence upon evoking the gifts of lay people. Her continual reference to the Holy Spirit caused some apprehension at first but soon pointed to the true source of Christian unity which they were experiencing.

The ideas and feeling which flowed from this ecumenical team provided the incentive for developing a variety of new person-centered programs. "Alphabet soup" characterizes the labels assigned to the six ecumenical experiments: IDEA, NIP, JHEM, C.Y.F., AYM, and NEM (pronounced "neem" as in "seem"). Some skeptics thought that the first year of training for this kind of community ministry would consist of an introduction to the new terminology. Most observers were amazed at the record-breaking speed with which these projects developed.

Whereas the first phase of the ecumenical adventure resulted from aggressive clergy initiation, the second phase of the process was identified with an expanded role for numerous lay persons. The first phase was primarily an expression of organizational development in contrast to the second phase, which added the dimension of personal growth. The transition was most apparent in the variety of ways that lay persons were trained for this new style of ministry.

Lay Leader Development

The initial emphasis upon community action was followed by a period of biblical reflection. The program which gave expression to this biblical emphasis was a six-week study series in the winter of 1966 called "Interfaith Dialogue for Ecumenical Action" (IDEA). Forty people from the four churches met weekly during most of February and March. Instead of the usual impersonal references to St. Patrick's, St. Anthony's, Christ Presbyterian, and Lake Avenue Baptist churches, members of these congregations got to know each other for the first time on a more intimate level. A study of the Biblical foundation for social action[1] was a means

---

[1] The resource used for this interfaith dialogue was George Younger's *The Bible Calls for Action* (Valley Forge: Judson Press, 1959).

to the end of discovering a deeper experience of Christian community. An awareness of what had happened was evident at the citywide Ecumenical Worship Service at the Eastman Theatre on March 27. Protestants and Catholics from the Edgerton Area realized that they had a new appreciation for each other that surpassed the routine contact with others of their own faith. When the lights were turned out after the service at the Eastman Theatre, the engrossed group of IDEA members on the aisle realized that they were left almost alone in the empty theatre. The gift of community was expressed more fully in several other new programs.

During the course of involving some church members in community action and biblical reflection, another group from the four churches was coalescing around an interest in youth ministry. The initial contact with the youth was made by two students from the Divinity School, assigned to Christ Presbyterian Church, who provided several new youth programs. Gradually they discovered a few key lay persons who shared their concern. These two students developed a style of "street ministry" in which they went to the street corners or snack shops where the teenagers gathered in natural groupings. In order to get a deeper level of relationship with the neighborhood youth, it was decided to have a "winter weekend" at the Penfield Rotary Club on January 7-9, 1966. This weekend was sponsored by Lake Avenue Baptist and Christ Presbyterian churches in cooperation with St. Anthony's and Holy Rosary churches. When asked what the churches in the area could do for them, the neighborhood youth said: "You can provide us with a place where we can meet together since we are not permitted to lounge around in the local restaurants." Shortly thereafter, a teen lounge was opened under a student's direction in the basement of Christ Presbyterian Church. The youth called it "The Place." An initial staff of fifteen lay persons was recruited from area churches in order to be present with the youth both at the lounge and on the street. The close relationships that developed between staff members and the neighborhood youth (many of whom were high school dropouts) provided at least a positive image of the church. Lay training was taken seriously from the beginning since the staff consisted largely of volunteers from the area churches. The staff evaluation sessions that took place after hours undergirded the newly formed Area Youth Ministry (AYM) with a sense of supportive community.

The challenge of this kind of involvement is reflected in the comments of a suburban housewife, one of the original seven staff members from the Lake Avenue Church:

I started participating in AYM with most of the conventional middle-class suburban concepts—both about the kids we would be working with at "The Place" and about my role in the ministry as a lay person. I felt that there wasn't much we could do for the kids beyond the "police keeping" function. I didn't believe it possible that a person of my background could establish a relationship with a delinquent youngster. And yet, somehow . . . this very relationship has come about. Once I became involved, I found myself carrying the burdens of the kids right along with them. I am very often aware that I can't solve their problems; but I know that their situation is less weighty because they know I care.

It is essential to me that there is an experienced street worker, a psychiatric social worker, and a theological person on the staff. I rely upon them to gain insight and understanding, to support or alter my thoughts or actions. It is also important that other lay staff members share with me their own sense of indecision, inadequacy, discouragement, or elation so that I am reminded of our common bond of human frailty.

Basically, involvement in this youth ministry has been more challenging to me than any other church work. We are dealing directly with people rather than raising money so that someone else can do it. The work is unique because we must work and think within a different cultural pattern which is foreign and threatening to us. The challenge is greater because we must use a relationship in order to achieve the desired results. In such a relationship, we as well as the kids, are affected. We are forced to look at ourselves—our convictions and attitudes—and find imperfection. This work, for example, has brought me to recognize the need for more mature religious understanding. I still have many doubts, but without this challenge I might still be coasting along . . . doubting, but doing nothing about it.[2]

[2] *Lake Avenue Church News* (March 22, 1967), published by the Lake Avenue Baptist Church, 57 Ambrose Street, Rochester, N.Y.

The existence of an ecumenical staff of thirty lay persons from eleven churches provided a base for supportive community in which they could gain confidence in reaching out to troubled youth. The emphasis was put on listening in a non-judgmental way and "sticking" with them through whatever consequence their actions brought.

By February, 1967, AYM had chosen their first full-time director. When the old building of Christ Presbyterian Church was being torn down to make way for a new building designed as a multipurpose community facility, the location of "The Place" was shifted to Dewey Avenue Presbyterian Church. It was a new concept of community ministry for Lake Avenue Church members to be deeply involved in a neighborhood program housed in Presbyterian churches and jointly staffed by Roman Catholics and Protestants. The larger community concern which developed within AYM was also expressed through a similar ministry with neighborhood children.

The new ecumenical style of community ministry set up the possibility for a new approach to the separate summer programs in the Edgerton Area. Previously Christ Presbyterian Church had conducted a successful vacation church school; St. Patrick's Church had a long tradition of summer school; Lake Avenue Church had a day camp program; and St. Anthony's Church had sponsored occasional recreational activities. As an extension of the Lenten Bible study series, the four coordinators mentioned previously started planning for an ecumenical alternative to vacation church school in the spring of 1966. The result was the Neighborhood Interfaith Program (NIP).[3]

NIP '66 was acknowledged as "the first interdenominational [Bible] school [for children] in the Rochester Diocese."[4] The

[3] Ruth M. Thunn, "Meet the Nippers" in *Baptist Leader* (October, 1967), pp. 22-23, gives a description of NIP '66 from the viewpoint of the children who participated in it. Cf. William R. Nelson, "An Ecumenical Alternative to Vacation Church School" in *Baptist Leader* (July, 1969), pp. 16-17, for a report of the expansion from NIP '66 to NIP '68 from the standpoint of a theologically trained educator.

[4] Joan Mancuso, "Baptist, Presbyterians, Catholics—Neighborhood Religion School," *The Catholic Courier Journal* (August 19, 1966), p. 5. Cf. William R. Nelson, "The Covenant of God in History" in *God's Doing–Man's Undoing,* edited by Ralph H. Elliott (Valley Forge: Judson Press, 1967), pp. 45-66, for a theological presentation of the "Salvation History" theme of NIP '66.

enthusiasm of the staff and children set in motion a process which continued to develop during subsequent summers. Although statistics only tell part of the story, a comparison of the first three summers looks like the spontaneous expansion of the early church.

	NIP '66	NIP '67	NIP '68
Sponsoring Churches	4	4	8
Lay Volunteers	40	125	250
Children	175	350	700
Buildings Used	1	3	5

Each summer the program was held during the four weeks of August for a total of twelve mornings (Tuesdays, Wednesdays, and Thursdays only). It was much easier to recruit busy housewives when Mondays and Fridays were left free. The four-week period was long enough to experience a sense of community in each of the classes from kindergarten through sixth grade. Classes were limited to fourteen children who were guided by a team of three teachers (usually two adults and one teenager). An extensive training program was held for the staff in June and July so that they could experience Christian community before attempting to share it with the children. Each teacher was asked to sign a "commitment form" indicating the extent of her involvement so that substitutes could be scheduled in advance whenever necessary.

A major breakthrough was in the area of curriculum. A three-year cycle was projected and developed which would enable urban children to identify with the experiences of key biblical characters. Creative drama was used to help the children discover the relevance of these past experiences for their present situation in the city. Because of the broader base of cooperation among four and eventually eight churches, there were enough people with talent in curriculum writing, drama, craft work, music, and administration to develop the entire program at the local level. An overview of the curriculum plan may be suggestive to other churches who are developing ecumenical resources.

	First Year	Second Year	Third Year
THEME:	Salvation History	Christian Community	Serving the World
CONTENT:	GOD CALLS US	RESPONSE IN COMMUNITY	RESPONSE IN THE WORLD

WEEK I:	God Chooses Abraham (Genesis 12, 21, 22)	God Calls Us Together (Matthew 4 and 9)	The World: Japan and Africa (Acts 2)
WEEK II:	God Works His Salvation Through Moses (Exodus 3, 12, 14)	Forgiving One Another (Luke 15; Matthew 18)	The City: Italian and Spanish-speaking (Acts 3)
WEEK III:	God Reconciles Us Through Christ's Sacrifice (Luke 24)	Sharing with One Another (Luke 17; Matthew 14)	Christian Community: Black Church (Acts 6–7)
WEEK IV:	God Affirms Us Through the Holy Spirit (Acts 2)	Serving One Another (Luke 15)	Our Response to God's Call (Acts 9)

The new ecumenical resource which emerged locally has been shared with other interested churches in Rochester and elsewhere. Their refinements have contributed to the process.

A by-product of the summer program was a revitalizing of interest in the Community Center at the Lake Avenue Church. The teenage members of the summer staff saw the value of continuing the same kind of biblical program on a less formal basis during the regular school year through the Community Center. Pat Murphy, one of Lake Avenue's urban trainees from the Divinity School, enabled the youth from the area churches to assume full responsibilty for continuing the ministry with neighborhood children. This new mission to the community for church-related youth from the four Edgerton churches provided the impetus for forming a Christian Youth Fellowship (C.Y.F.). The experience of one of the younger laity from the Lake Avenue Church is described:

I became interested in the Community Center because of my participation in NIP during the summer of 1966. Although the majority of the forty teachers were adults, there were about eight teenage helpers. Through this summer program I got to know many children, especially my third-grade class. When the teenagers of the Edgerton churches responded to the challenge of providing leadership for the

Community Center, I asked to work with the fourth-grade class and was glad to see them again when the Community Center opened on December 3, 1966. (It took us about a month to get our staff organized and to plan our curriculum after we decided to accept the responsibility for the Community Center on October 23.) All of the thirty teachers are teenagers this time, and they come from the Protestant and Roman Catholic churches of the Edgerton Area. Some of them have taken this responsibility more seriously than others, but everyone has done something—even if it is just to show the children that we care enough about them to come every Saturday morning.

I have found out many things about myself in relation to the teenagers I work with and the children I teach. I learned that the children do not behave as well for me as they did during the summer when there were adults around, but it's more of a challenge this way. I found out that some of the teenagers were a little bit hard to become acquainted with, but when I really tried to make friends, it wasn't so hard. Most important of all, I learned that the people I work with and the children I teach are just as good as any of my other friends. I may have a few more material things than some of them, but we share the most important things in common, such as the desire for happiness and the feeling of mutual trust. In the last few months I've found out what real friends are, I've learned about a new side of life, and it means more to me than you could ever imagine.[5]

As long as the emphasis was on the common task of working with neighborhood children, the C.Y.F. flourished. But it was difficult to sustain this kind of involvement. Murphy's emphasis was upon enabling the group to use their own talents more creatively. His departure during the summer of 1967 took the pressure off in terms of community ministry. Thereafter the C.Y.F. became more of a fellowship and less of a mission-oriented service group. The participation of teenagers from the Lake Avenue Church was always limited to about six persons. Many parents resented the loss of a fellowship group within their church for the many teenagers who were not involved in C.Y.F.

[5] *Lake Avenue Church News* (April 5, 1967).

A student minister who was assigned to the Lake Avenue Church by the Divinity School was given the difficult assignment of trying to revive the defunct Sunday Night Club. He felt that involvement in community ministry might give the few survivors of this fellowship group for single young adults a reason to exist. The same mission-oriented approach was also presented to a similar group from Bethany Presbyterian Church. Together the two churches recruited about ten young adults who volunteered their service to begin a junior high program at St. Patrick's Church in Brown Square. With the help of Sister Rose, a few Roman Catholic lay persons were added to the core group of Protestants to form the Junior High Ecumenical Ministry (JHEM). A coffeehouse was opened in the basement of St. Patrick's Church which provided a point of contact with many restless youth in Brown Square. The shift from the church building to a public facility is described by a single young man from the Lake Avenue Church.

When I became a member of the staff of JHEM, I did not realize that I would get so involved. Now that I have learned more about these kids, I find myself so concerned and interested in them that I want to be with them several times a week. It all started last fall when some single young adults accepted the challenge to engage in a ministry with the junior high youth of Brown Square. Our first venture was to start a coffeehouse in the basement of St. Patrick's Church so that we could get to know the kids better. The facilities at the coffeehouse included a Ping-Pong table, music turned to their liking, refreshments, and games. For myself, this informal approach was the best way to get involved with these kids. When some damage to the building caused the coffeehouse to be closed down after four weeks, we realized that it was not an end in itself but a means to the end of getting to know the kids. This crisis helped us to see beyond the housekeeping chores of a particular program and gave us an opportunity to reaffirm our basic commitment to a ministry with junior high youth.

For the past four months we have been working in and through the Brown Square Recreation Center. Since we no longer had a program to maintain, our emphasis has been on street ministry, that is, being with the kids on the street where they spend a great deal of their time. The recreation center is a good springboard for these informal contacts. Through this experience I have discovered that these kids are demanding that I be honest and sincere. I have learned that they will act human only when they are treated as such. They do not want to be put into any mold by their parents or society. I have also learned that the wilder their behavior, the louder their cry for help. This whole experience has been one of great value to me. I have learned more about myself and about others, especially how to love those who are different from me. The whole staff is gaining a new perspective on teenagers, and the opportunity of working with these kids has given our group a reason for existence.[6]

The original junior high group in Brown Square found another core group of lay persons working with junior highs at Christ Presbyterian Church. When St. Patrick's Church was no longer available, these two groups merged. They began a coffeehouse, "The Cellar," in the basement of St. Anthony's Church.

The vacuum left by the closing of "The Place" and the need for more training of the JHEM staff led to a cooperative relationship with AYM, their senior high counterpart. AYM had shifted its program away from the original coffeehouse approach emphasizing individual relationships to an action-orientation consisting of task forces dealing with the political structures which affect youth. In addition to task forces dealing with dropouts, with jails and probation officers, with courts and welfare agencies, with employers and schools, AYM was also the moving force behind the formation of a city-wide coalition for training workers with youth called "RISK." [7] Regular seminars were held on drugs, white racism, the judicial system, and welfare problems at the RISK Institute located in Nazareth College. The focus of this specialized training was on equipping the laity for ministry rather than depending exclusively upon professionals. The lay persons related to the JHEM staff were able to take advantage of this training too. Whereas JHEM continued to operate within a building, AYM was developing an understanding for the secular institutions affecting city youth.

[6] *Lake Avenue Church News* (March 29, 1967).

[7] Lincoln Richardson, "Rochester's Ministry to Youth," *Presbyterian Life* (January 15, 1969), pp. 22-23.

The polarity of organizational development and personal growth goals has already been hinted at in the contrast between E.A.N.A. and IDEA. As long as the organizational effort was aimed at social change, there was more emphasis upon object-oriented goals. When the organizational effort was aimed at personal growth, object-oriented goals were naturally replaced by person-centered goals (such as the cultivation of new relationships in IDEA). This shift was made completely by NIP where the emphasis upon Christian community provided an environment of personal enrichment both for the children and the teen/adult staff.

The turn of events in AYM took exactly the opposite direction. Although beginning with person-centered goals at "The Place," the complexity of problems confronting the staff called for something more. The emphasis gradually shifted to object-oriented goals which were implemented by various task forces. The social structures affecting youth became the target of this organizational development process. The inclination toward social action was reinforced by the director and key lay staff members. Pressure from other lay staff members resulted in a modified return to person-centered goals with the opening of a Drop-In Center in the new building of Christ Presbyterian Church on May 1, 1969. Its purpose was to be responsive to individual youth by offering assistance with information and resources which were not ordinarily at their disposal. One or two lay staff members were present each night with several others on call. There was a conscious attempt to discourage recreation or social gatherings. This approach had only a limited appeal and was not as popular as expected. It was generally interpreted as a move to pacify the disgruntled staff members who objected to the closing of "The Place." The political action emphasis continued to develop under the leadership of the youth themselves through a group called Concerned Youth.

The other two programs, JHEM and C.Y.F., were not as highly polished as either NIP or AYM, but their purpose pointed in the direction of personal growth. Whether it was single young adults working with neighborhood senior highs or church-related senior highs working with neighborhood children, the main value resulted from personal enrichment both to those giving of themselves and those receiving from others.

The internal organizational struggle of separate ecumenical projects has been described in considerable detail. Instead of leaving each group alone to find its own way, the formation of an overall coordination unit for ecumenical mission in the northwest sector seemed essential. In the winter of 1967-1968 a proposal was drafted by Nelson, Booher, Russell, and several others to form the Northwest Ecumenical Ministry (NEM). By subdividing the sector into three planning units (Maplewood, Edgerton, and Otis), local neighborhood involvement was encouraged. The NEM board also provided a direct link with the strategy and funding guidelines of the Board for Urban Ministry of the Rochester Area Council of Churches and the Urban Ministry Office of the Rochester Roman Catholic Diocese. Most important of all, the NEM board formalized the lay participation in the ecumenical process by calling for officially designated lay and clergy representatives of the member churches.

Just as the Northwest Clergy Association was the key to the first phase of the expanding community ministry, NEM was the outgrowth of the second stage in which lay leader development was emphasized. Each of the three subcommunities had a planning council made up of two laymen and a clergyman from each participating church. The chairman of each planning unit, plus one representative (lay or clergy) from each congregation, made up the NEM board. The inclusion of lay persons at the decision-making level in the development of priorities for the total mission of the church in the northwest sector was a significant step forward.

The growing enthusiasm associated with an ecumenical approach to community ministry is reflected in a progress report made by Dr. George Hill to urban churchmen of the American Baptist Convention:

> The original commitment of Lake Avenue Baptist Church was to an ecumenical ministry. We stand solidly on the platform that you can't deal with the multi-faceted problems of the community on a narrow denominational base. You simply have to reach out to all men who share your commitment to Jesus Christ and work in this largest possible human context.
>
> Now we have institutionalized our ecumenical commitment. When the four churches which are at the center of the Edgerton area turn to their own constituencies, they respond according to their own specific traditions. But when these four churches look outwardly to the community, they are now one church in the most literal sense you can imagine. We finance, plan, staff and implement what we do as one church.
>
> What this means is that we departmentalize the mission activity. The

work with neighborhood children centers at Lake Avenue Baptist Church. At the junior high level the ministry centers at St. Patrick's Church. The senior high involvement centers in Christ Presbyterian Church. At the adult level the program centers at St. Anthony's Church.[8]

Freedom to Fail

The record-breaking speed with which the new route of local community ministry developed was unquestionably a success story at the end of the second year of the experiment.[9] However, three warning signs pointed to the possibility of trouble ahead on this ecclesiastical speedway: (1) a growing feeling of discontent was developing among the more traditional members of the Lake Avenue Church; (2) two key persons subsequently faded away from the ecumenical scene; (3) a sense of rebellion against church control of its mission projects was developing in Brown Square.

It is difficult for a church to be all things to all people. Under the leadership of Dr. Hill, Lake Avenue Church had chosen to be a prophetic voice for social change in the metropolitan area. The new route for expressing this passion for social justice was found to be within a one-mile radius of its imposing Gothic sanctuary. The newly renovated educational building was being used to serve a variety of neighborhood groups. The number of church members involved in these programs had increased from twenty-five during the first six months to well over one hundred by the end of the second year. The strong preaching ministry of Dr. Hill tended to give the impression that internal fellowship and mutual

---

[8] *Creative Ministry 15,* "The Rochester Story: A Panel Presentation by Harvey A. Everett, George W. Hill, William R. Nelson, and Ray Kicklighter" (American Baptist Home Mission Societies, Valley Forge, Pa. 19481, May 19, 1967), p. 6. Cf. Stephen C. Rose, *The Grass Roots Church* (New York: Holt, Rinehart and Winston, 1966), pp. 67-95.

[9] Joan Thatcher, *The Church Responds* (Valley Forge: Judson Press, 1970), pp. 86-91, describes the initial success of the project by summarizing the new forms of ecumenical community ministry which developed during the first two years. To stop there is misleading because the subsequent developments in community ministry were characterized by failure more than success. In spite of a gradual loss of the initial momentum of ecumenical fervor, a more mature ecumenical structure did emerge in the Northwest Ecumenical Ministry. The ups and downs of that continuing process eliminate any tendency toward romanticizing the story.

support were authentic only when related specifically to the mission of the church in the world.

The gulf began to widen between the core group who were interested in ecumenical community ministry and the majority of church members whose concern was directed toward a variety of traditional mission projects, such as mission supply, hospital service, literacy work, and shut-in visitation. The larger group resented all the attention that was directed to one aspect of the church's ministry and began to feel like "second-class citizens of the kingdom." Except for the persistent preaching about secular involvement and the personal exposure of selected members to community ministry, the rest of the congregational life was quite traditional.

—Participation at Sunday morning worship services had been declining steadily for many years.
—There was a traditional church school program with a pattern of declining attendance.
—The leadership core was diminishing so that key positions were rotated among a relatively small group.
—The number of new members was falling behind the annual membership loss.
—Budget needs were constantly increasing to stay ahead of the rising cost of living.

Therefore, a casual visitor could pass through the worship service on Sunday morning without catching the new spirit of experimentation that was developing for the most part outside the walls of the building. Only those who took the trouble to attend an adult class in the church school or to participate in specific weekday projects would have learned about the unprecedented opportunities for community ministry.

The initial success of the ecumenical approach to community ministry was largely due to the personal influence of four key people. They found in each other a glimpse of Christian community which seemed to be lacking in their respective congregations or parishes. Each in his or her own way tried to enable this kind of experience among others. Yet it soon became apparent that God had other plans for two members of this ecumenical team.

Father Russell began to have informal discussions and mass in the homes of St. Anthony's parishioners. His attempts to be a real person who was faced with doubts and uncertainties left most of his Italian parishioners bewildered. They expected him to be an ecclesiastical professional who had all the right answers. As his liberal views about racial justice and peace became known more widely, he became a threat to the more conservative orientation of the parish. His popularity in the community was beginning to fade when a tragic accident caused by monoxide poisoning aroused the sympathy of even his most avid foes. Russell recovered completely. He resumed his full duties several months after the accident and again attempted to relate on a personal level. However, his concern was interpreted as "meddling with the private affairs of his parishioners." As a result of this and because of various other reasons, he decided to leave the active priesthood. He accepted a position with an insurance company as the arena for his continuing witness to Christ.

Sister Rose Vincent found her primary parochial identity with the Legion of Mary. Her quiet, non-assuming manner was the spiritual force which enabled about six dedicated lay persons to carry on a regular program of parish visitation. Yet it was the quiet time of prayer and the informal discussions of selected Scripture passages which sustained them in this thankless task among the residents of Brown Square.

Unlike Father Russell, Sister Rose tried to work under a pastor who did not share her enthusiasm for ecumenism. The extent of cooperation from St. Patrick's Church was never more than the reluctant use of the building and minimal financial support. As the gap between pastor and nun continued to widen, he finally requested that she be transferred to another city. Her decision to go back to college and complete her formal education in the field of psychology provided a temporary diversion from her ecclesiastical disillusionment. She has since left the Trinitarian order and set her mind on a career as a psychiatric social worker.

In reflecting on her two-year sojourn in Brown Square, she said: "The tragedy at St. Anthony's resulted in a cooling off of the Roman Catholic support for ecumenism in the area. When the key Catholic church became immobilized without its priests, it seemed undeniable that ecumenism had been forced from the top instead of emerging from leaders in the parish. In this respect it was like 'fool's gold.'" The implication of her comment is that phase one of clergy initiation was much more successful than phase two of lay leader development. Instead of the clergy acting unilaterally, phase two at least represented an attempt to include lay persons in the decision-making process. Yet it was unmistakable that the clergy were still "at the wheel." The short-term life span of about two years for IDEA, C.Y.F., and JHEM seemed to reinforce this bureaucratic tendency. Nevertheless, the continuing development of NIP and AYM pointed to a deeper bond which was formalized in the Northwest Ecumenical Ministry. Although the original spark of discovery could not be sustained indefinitely, there was a maturing process of consolidation in which the best features of the initial experimentation were conserved.

The inability of Brown Square residents to fit into the new ecumenical programs has been mentioned previously. The gnawing anxiety which came from the poor was the fear of church control which would deprive them of the opportunity for self-help. This reservation led to the development of an alternative style of community organization under Lincoln's leadership. The new route for Brown Square became known as WEDGE, a community development corporation which took its name from an industrial tool for change. The contrast may be sharpened by summarizing the varying degrees of church control which were discernible in the early years of the experiment.

—It is to be expected that *church-sponsored ecumenical ministries* would be planned, implemented, and controlled by church bodies. The most significant developments in this category were the children's summer Bible school (NIP), the sector-wide action-oriented youth ministry (AYM), and eventually the sector-wide planning and strategy group (NEM).

—The gray area was found in a *quasi-church group* like E.A.N.A. in which church control was minimized at best but was nevertheless present.

—The other option was found in a *non-church group* like WEDGE which insisted upon a secular identity while utilizing the resources of the church in a supportive role.

The new route originated from the community itself. The story of this alternative approach to community ministry will be described in the next three chapters.

Looking Ahead to Chapter 5

Too often the church professes a philosophy which is inconsistent with its performance. Such was the case with Lake Avenue Church. While performing the prophetic function as a political advocate for rapid social change, it neglected pastoral responsibilities to the poor and powerless. Seldom did it have any personal contact with the actual victims of the urban crisis. By becoming immersed in the problems of the church's changing community, Lincoln sought to develop a pastoral ministry in Brown Square, a so-called "poverty area" located only a few blocks from the church. Chapter 5 entitled "Unexpected Detour" describes his initial involvement in the area as a significant departure from the clergy-dominated ecumenical approach to community ministry.

5   Unexpected Detour

After a frustrating attempt to work within the existing community center program at the Lake Avenue Church, Lincoln was asked to learn more about this Brown Square community. His strong interest in social work also caused him to feel the need to become personally involved with the church's immediate neighborhood. Nelson, who was at least technically Lincoln's supervisor, thought that his nonconformist tendencies could be channeled more creatively in an unstructured situation. The initial experience of this restless seminarian in Brown Square reflects the painful development which all urban ministers must undergo.

At first Lincoln concentrated on getting a feeling for the physical characteristics of the neighborhood. It is adorned with the splendor of the Eastman Kodak Company headquarters, several businesses with attractive exteriors, and a substantial number of homes owned by elderly Italians who daily sweep cracked sidewalks and prune small flower gardens. Overpowering this minimal beauty are large junkyards, blocks of vacant stores, abandoned cars on vacant lots, empty buildings, deteriorating multiple dwellings, and trash-ridden streets. The only physical assets which provide centers for community activity are Elementary School #5, a well-equipped playground in Brown Square Park, a Spanish-speaking Pentecostal church, and St. Patrick's Church.

It was much more difficult to get a clear picture of the people living in the area. The city's 1963 Community Renewal Program described the area in these general terms: "Adult education levels below average; unemployment high; above average percentage of renter-occupancy; average to very high vacancy ratio; high degree of deterioration and dilapidation." The population is primarily composed of Italians with an increasing number of Puerto Ricans and Negroes. There are signs that this section of the city might soon become a main port of entry into Rochester by non-whites, or serve as a harbor for those dislocated by urban renewal programs in other neighborhoods. The city's Department of Urban Renewal and Economic Development once recommended that the entire 208 acres be used for "controlled" industry (eventually calling for the relocation of five hundred to eight hundred families) and that Elementary School #5 be converted into a new vocational high school.

Plunge into Poverty

Lincoln was foolishly optimistic that these urban dwellers would welcome him gladly. With the naiveté of a young and inexperienced divinity school student, he armed himself with Christian love and walked into *their* community to serve *his* God. Because of the ambiguous nature of his assignment ("listen to the community"), he detached himself from the institutional church and entered the world of the unattached. For several months he walked the streets with fleeing enthusiasm. If queried by fellow students, faculty, or staff from the church, he unhesitatingly produced fictitious incidents, reports, and plans which were compatible with their stereotyped view of this form of ministry. In disgust with himself and this apparently God-forsaken community, he would purchase cigarettes from a local market or find some retreat outside the community in which to sip coffee for hours. Each time he departed from the church with inspiring enthusiasm only to return in total dejection. And so the process went from hostility to guilt, to depression, and finally to a focus on reality.

It was late one Saturday afternoon that his walk became distinctly different from all previous wanderings. For some reason this time his senses were not oblivious to the environment but absorbed its realities like a dry porous sponge. Lying in the dust by a vacant corner lot near the old subway bed was an empty aluminum foiled pack which once contained a prophylactic. In the general area within ten feet his eyes caught signs of love's discards: empty beer cans, cigarette butts, lipstick blotted tissues, and finally the limp form of the used condom. Stereotypes were broken, and *conditions were personified.*

Then he scanned uncut lawns, peeling paint, broken windows, sagging porches, padlocked mailboxes, torn screens, abandoned automobiles, and many proud yet hurting people. He heard blaring radios, wailing babies, screaming mothers, yelping dogs, and foul cursing from a tavern accompanied by the response of a Spanish tongue and the laughs of children. He smelled pizza, sausage, exotic spices, and strange unidentifiable odors from decaying junk and garbage, including occasional sniffs of urine as he passed through cluttered alleys. That afternoon he finally realized that he was in the midst of many poor, dispossessed, ignored, and forgotten people—a reservoir of untapped resource. Such walks he found necessary in developing the lamest of ministries into a confident and effective stride.

For the remainder of that year Lincoln entered into a "participation-observation" method of social research and involvement. It consisted of his purchasing gasoline from a small Esso station located behind the Kodak Tower and cigarettes in a congested Italian market. He had his clothes cleaned at a small tuxedo shop and then ate lunch at a dinette across from St. Patrick's Church. Occasionally he would drink beer in some small bar and grill, purchase pizza for home consumption from Giuseppe's by the playground or fresh bread from one of several neighborhood bakeries. This participation-observation was a "reconnaissance— an initial exploration of a community to provide an overview." [1] It took place through using the facilities and services of Brown Square, such as dropping in at the playground, attending various affairs at St. Patrick's, and chatting informally with people in shops and homes.

"Participation-observation" as a form of Christian ministry presupposes a truism which is often overlooked—the need to honestly remain ourselves at all times, in all places, and in all circumstances. It was encouraging to learn that William Stringfellow found no need to repudiate his culture or personal history while in Harlem. [2]

Unfortunately, the church often hinders inner-city ministry by perpetuating the common fallacy that identification with people comes only through imitation of their customs, mannerisms, and even style of dress. Such pretension is regarded by the people whom we hope to serve as artificial if not bitter mockery. In spite

[1] Herbert J. Gans, *The Urban Villagers* (New York: The Free Press, 1962), p. 350.

[2] William Stringfellow, *My People Is the Enemy* (New York: Holt, Rinehart and Winston, 1964), p. 27.

of good intentions, it can be a morally dishonest attempt to fool people who have been fooled for years and who have learned through disappointing experiences to spot a facade efficiently and accurately. If we accept ourselves, then there is no need for us to hide from, or apologize for our educational level or socioeconomic status. The poor expect us to be somewhat differently equipped if we are to be of any resourcefulness in helping them out of their predicament. Neither do we need to be casual and pleasant toward the horror of their existence. More than impotent sympathy, people want and need honesty in the form of our genuine presence and concern. Consequently, Lincoln learned he could buy another's drink or refuse someone's offer to purchase his, wear either a white shirt and tie or frayed and faded khakis, joke one moment with a family or raise his voice to them in the next, visit two hours or just casually chat by the hedge for mere seconds. The risk in adhering to the old romantic idea of detached ministry is the unreality of artificial over-identificaton which will result in total ineffectiveness.

During the winter and spring of 1966, Lincoln was invited by Sister Rose to participate in the lay apostolic work of the Legion of Mary at St. Patrick's Church. Each Monday evening a dozen people would gather to recite the Rosary, study Scripture, offer prayer, and discuss their assigned visitations within the community. Admittedly this ecumenical relationship was strategically valuable during his initial efforts in Brown Square. The latent advantages of participation in the Legion resulted in some identification with the Catholic church, increased community contacts, and strengthened relationships with the few people whom he had already met on his own. It must be made clear, however, that he approached this new experience without any hidden agenda. He and Sister Rose often had frank exchanges which were made possible only by a unique openness between them, a spiritual fondness toward one another, and a mutually shared concern for the people in their common parish. Neither of them sought to become "ecumaniacs." They only wished to serve the people with whom they found themselves. Lincoln readily admitted that he would never forget her influence upon his own personal life and ministry and still remains indebted to her for the strength with which she supported him when he gazed at the community in futile despair. Her unpretentious style represented the epitome of messianic character. She emptied herself into service with people and then crept away unnoticed in order, as she used to say, "that the Holy Spirit may perform his work unmolested by my human desire for recognition."

During the same time Lincoln also participated in the formation of the Edgerton Area Neighborhood Association whose boundaries then included the Brown Square community. The purpose of any community organization is to "organize the residents of the community so they can take a positive role in planning for the inevitable changes which are certain to occur." [3] Meeting after meeting, however, gave evidence that most Brown Square residents were not participating in that organization, and the few who were had little knowledge of what it was basically all about. Street work and door knocking were intensified to increase and strengthen interpersonal relationships with neighborhood residents, a definite prerequisite for community organizers.

Not until late spring of 1966 did Lincoln actually begin to respond to people's needs. His help was at first of an emergency nature. A nineteen-year-old Puerto Rican boy with whom he had recently become well acquainted was seriously stabbed by another Puerto Rican youth. While visiting the victim in the hospital, he learned that the stabbed youth was concerned about his assailant whom he described as one of "his people." Now there was no time for fear or reluctance on his part since immediate action was needed. How the situation ultimately terminated is not important. What cannot be ignored is that mysterious yet conscious commitment which led Lincoln to police headquarters, detective offices, the home of the victim, the penitentiary, a bondsman, lawyers, and finally the courts. At the home of the imprisoned youth he was finally able to accept bare-bottomed children, fly-ridden tables, the stench of human waste, and evidence of apparent incest. All that mattered was that people were in trouble and at that moment only he was in the position to offer some relief—an awesome feeling of responsibility and helplessness.

The transition from the school year to the summer recess allowed Lincoln needed time to reflect upon and to analyze the meaning of his personal involvement in a poverty area. A con-

[3] Lyle E. Schaller, *Community Organization: Conflict and Reconciliation* (Nashville: Abingdon Press, 1966), p. 35. Cf. Robert Lee and Russell Galloway, *The Schizophrenic Church: Conflict over Community Organization* (Philadelphia: The Westminster Press, 1969).

stantly recurring thought was that he was approaching this type of ministry with the wrong emotion. Christianity's sentimental attachment to John 3:16 is too often subverted by our shallow understanding of reciprocal love between men. This heart-warming text means little to many beaten people who are either unattached to the church or who are so theologically illiterate that even a compulsive church attendance might only provide an unrealistic and false hope that things will be better tomorrow. To many the church is not a reference point since the hope and love it proclaims is as ambiguous as the Beatitudes. When an unemployed father leaves his household in order that his family might obtain increased welfare payments, when a child has to play on the curb of a congested street because of the rats in his yard, when a mother must carry buckets of water up three stories from the basement because the pressure in her plumbing only spits drops, and when a good-income Negro family is refused admittance to a part of town in which they want and can afford to live, it is difficult to talk about Christian love.

These people are aware of the reality displayed by Amos's plumb line which exposes the obvious inequalities of society (cf. Amos 7:7-8). Consequently, they are more knowledgeable of hate than love. Could it not be a time for *Christian hate* toward injustice in place of superficial love? Are poor people not justified in hating the symbols which cause their misery? The poor always see evil personified, and it is to these symbolic people that they direct their anger. Jesus, of course, never implied sanction of personal hate even for retaliation. It was love toward all which he admonished. Nevertheless, Lincoln learned from the poor with grateful appreciation how easy it is for one to hate his oppression as well as his oppressor. His challenge was to redirect this hatred of people toward the symbols of injustice and the causes of poverty. Only then would it be possible to take seriously Amos's plea to hate evil and love good, Jesus' command to love our enemies, and Tillich's insistence that love has a strange quality of despising all that exists against righteousness.

The undeniable existence of poverty in the community adjacent to the Lake Avenue Church added a reality focus to the possibility of demonstrating Christian love in the midst of extreme human need. The kind of picture which became imprinted in the consciousness of some of the more sensitive persons in the congregation may be grasped through a series of flashbacks. These portraits of poverty represent isolated individuals living in the Brown Square community who were once largely unknown to each other. The bond which they shared in common was a mutual trust for Lincoln, their "community chaplain" whose presence in the neighborhood meant that somebody cared.

Portrait of Loneliness

Every poor community seems to have at least one personality who colorfully exemplifies the white stereotype of Uncle Remus. "Mr. Bill," as he was affectionately called by both children and adults, was a seventy-year-old Negro who suffered from acute loneliness. A train accident in Georgia some forty years ago resulted in the amputation of his left leg, dismissal from railroad employment without any compensation, and divorce from his wife. By way of track camps and flop houses, he eventually arrived and settled in Rochester some fifteen years later. Living in a condemned building, he sustained himself by collecting rags and metals scavenged from residential and industrial trash. Each day he would limp upon his wooden leg throughout the community in search of treasures to be redeemed for bread and wine.

Although an alcoholic, he was never offensive or feared in the community. Residents still recall the countless hours he spent telling humorous tales to a curb audience of attentive children. In antiquated Southern tradition he would always rise, nod, and cordially greet any approaching white at the cost of his own pride. He *properly* addressed the smallest girls as "Miss" and the boys as "Master," utilizing their first name in all cases.

One winter day, Mr. Bill slipped and fell unnoticed in an alley not far from his residence. Several days later a black woman living in the same building discovered him lying unconscious, frostbitten, and bloody-faced in his unheated room. Medical care was sought with appalling results. White ambulance attendants refused to enter the smelly apartment, thus making it necessary for others to bundle and carry him downstairs to the vehicle. Several hours elapsed between his arrival at the hospital and the time he was actually seen by any doctor, nurse, or orderly. Upon being revived to semiconsciousness, he was given a bowl of soup and then sent home in a taxi.

By this time the case had come to the attention of Lincoln and several community leaders who together quickly rectified the situation. For nine months Mr. Bill convalesced in the county hospital and home for the aged. During this period adequate disability payments and other forms of governmental assistance were arranged for his permanent support. In addition, they were able to locate his married son who enthusiastically urged his father to come and live with him in Florida. No longer was Mr. Bill to be alone.

Portrait of Aimlessness

Dick had been long employed as an interior painter when he fell and suffered a serious back injury. Beyond his eligibility to receive benefits from various health insurance programs, he had no alternative to support himself and his family other than public assistance. The constant reassignment of his case to different social workers over a two-year period reinforced his growing dependence upon the welfare system. During this time he also became an effective parasite on every conceivable charity program in order to satisfy his compulsive materialism. At thirty-five, six years following the accident, he was ordered to secure full-time employment immediately. It was not until Dick's *ninth* social worker, who was sensitive to other people, acknowledged him to be psychologically unfit for the open job market, that he was able to enroll in a meaningful rehabilitation program.

Portrait of Despair

Sherry is a twenty-five-year-old white who has been unable to adjust to being an attractive young abandoned mother of two small children. In her attempts to become economically independent, she secured employment in two restaurants—one from 6:00 A.M. to 3:00 P.M., the other from 4:30 P.M. until 9:00 P.M. The income from the second job was spent for babysitting fees, transportation costs, and the expense of uniform care.

Despair prevailed as she became increasingly aggravated with her children's undisciplined behavior and her own exhaustion which prevented her from dealing with the problems of child-rearing. As these circumstances intensified, she became prey to men who expressed their admiration and desire for marriage. Two miscarriages and one pregnancy later—each differently fathered— have made her severely judgmental of herself and untrusting of everyone. No longer is she either discriminate about the character of her dates or concerned with their intentions. It's their ability to pay for her services which matters most to her now.

Portrait of Harassment

There exist countless instances of absentee landlords harassing assertive tenants who expect their apartments to comply with the basic building code: proper maintenance of plumbing, electrical wiring, and heating systems. Often landlords have intimidated such tenants by issuing forged court orders of eviction, illegally discontinuing necessary utilities, and threatening to report false or inflated reports of misconduct to social workers. And all too frequently, tenants have bowed to such pressure tactics. A ridiculous, yet somewhat humorous incident was endured by a former black community leader shortly after she was forced to relocate her residency from Brown Square to an even more impoverished neighborhood, Rochester's Model City Area. The following account appeared in a local newspaper, expect for the deletion of several names and addresses:

> Mrs. E. H. and her eight children were watching television last night when three strange men stopped by to take all the doors off their apartment. The men, Mrs. H. said, claimed they were working for the city. But as the family sat shivering in the blasts of 15-degree temperature blowing through the apartment, she decided she'd like to have her doors back.
>
> As it turned out, the men weren't working for the city, but rather for the landlord. When they returned the doors five hours later, at 11:30 P.M., one of the men, who refused to identify himself to anyone but police, actually was the landlord himself. When the landlord returned the doors, he said he really was representing the owner of the property. He said the owner had received a notice from the city to repair the doors within five days.
>
> This information was interesting to four men who had gathered in Mrs. H's apartment while the doors were gone: a director of property conservation, a city commissioner of building, an attorney from the Monroe County Bar Legal Assistance Corp., and an organizer for Rochester Action for Welfare Rights. These men were agreed that no such order had been issued to the landlord.[4]

Portrait of Injustice

Although Juan was a highly regarded butcher, he found it too difficult and expensive to become a union member. In an effort to

[4] Frank Zoretich, "The Doors: Who Has the Doors?" in *The Democrat and Chronicle* (Rochester, N.Y.: March 10, 1970). Used with permission.

supplement his income and provide better care for his wife and four children, he engaged in selling marijuana which, incidentally, appears to be no more prevalent in poor Puerto Rican and black communities than in highly respected white academic institutions. Later, he began to deal with heroin, a business venture condemned by almost everyone regardless of their socioeconomic level.

A county-wide raid resulted in the arrest of Juan and two dozen other such dealers. His apprehension and indictment were just; his conviction and sentencing were not. Defendants identically accused, but with financial and/or political resources, received reduced sentences and in some cases even acquittal. It seems that the same injustice prevails when it comes to acts of theft, assault, rape, or murder. Defendants having limited resources are more often convicted and draw heavier sentences than affluent offenders accused of identical crimes.

Equality and justice are the prerequisites for crime prevention and law and order. Inconsistent or arbitrary court rulings which continually favor one group over another make democracy into a sham. Juan, guilty by his own admission, wonders whether financial backing or political influence could have made a difference in his sentence.

Portrait of Inhumanity

Mrs. Hanson entered this country from Sweden as a happy young bride. Living on a moderate income, she and her husband raised two children, both of whom entered professional careers, married, and moved out of state. The death of her husband in an industrial accident made Mrs. Hanson a widow at forty-two. Upon her decision to remain in Rochester, she began dating a divorced taxicab driver.

Shortly after their marriage she realized him to be a sexual pervert and the owner of several houses of ill repute. An ensuing argument resulted in her being unmercifully beaten and confined to the house incommunicado. To assure his own self-protection, this man had his first wife and teenage daughters also move into the house where he managed their prostitution. Only after his fatal heart attack was it possible to assist this woman in actually escaping the situation. Her daughter invited her to live with her in the Midwest. Now at the age of fifty she is again living a happy life with part of her family.

Portrait of Racism

Tony is not any one person but denotes a substantially large category of Brown Square Italian residents who are resistant to all forms of social change. Tony is a long-term resident of the community, owns and maintains his property, drives a late model car, eats and dresses well. He lacks only one thing—the willingness to develop a compassionate understanding of the people caught in the circumstances which perpetuate poverty, especially racism and the moral judgment of others. Tony is the one who signed the petition demanding a young white mother to either give up her black child or move out of the neighborhood. He is the one who barred black and Puerto Rican welfare tenants from membership in an emerging neighborhood organization. He calls the police when two or three teenagers congregate on a street corner even though he realizes there is no other place for them to go. He opposes construction of low-income housing in the community and violently opposes a city-wide grade reorganization plan which would assure quality integrated education of all children in all schools. But Tony is preparing to leave for the suburbs to join the WASP's (White Anglo-Saxon Protestants), who share his views. It is hoped that many other longtime Italian residents of Brown Square who have actively demonstrated their concern for the community's poor and powerless will still be able to change Tony's attitude.

Additional cases could be given to portray *hunger* as seen in the two hundred families who receive government-issued surplus foods or the poor woman who steals vegetables from property owners' gardens. *Nakedness* can be seen in the raggedly dressed nine-year-old white girl who sifts through Monday morning's trash in search of shoes and other items of discarded clothing. *Ill health* could be easily documented by school absenteeism or trips to emergency wards for treatment of common illnesses; and many illustrations of substandard housing and unemployment could be given too. And, of course, Brown Square has its share of burglaries, rapes, murders, and suicides. In all these respects this neighborhood is no different from any other poor community in an intermediate-sized city, such as Rochester. Most of the people are tired and worn but warm and sincere in their treatment of each other. Anyone from the outside who becomes immersed in this or similar communities quickly gains a genuine respect for its people, their dietary habits, ethnic customs, and creative improvisations necessary for survival.

But wandering and wondering is not enough for the Christian. What are we to be? What are we to do? Do there have to be inequality and injustice? Does there have to be a "plumb line"? Do there have to be *in-groups* and *out-groups, we* and *they?* Kipling, although referring to the schism between East and West caused by ignorance and fear ("never the twain shall meet"), has a lesson for all who remain distant from our ghettoized brothers:

> All good people agree
>   And all good people say
> All nice people like Us, are We
>   And everyone else is They.
> But, if you cross over the sea
>   Instead of over the way,
> You may end by (think of it)
>   Looking on We
> As only a sort of They.[5]

Just who are the *people of God?* Lake Avenue Church was not quite sure, but it was at least becoming aware of the poor in its immediate community.

[5] Rudyard Kipling, "We and They," *Debits and Credits* (New York: Doubleday & Company, Inc., 1926). Reprinted by permission of Mrs. George Bambridge and Doubleday & Company, Inc.

Looking Ahead to Chapter 6

In order to serve the world effectively, the church must be willing to surrender its own self-preserving institutional interests. Unfortunately, congregational consensus and urban mission are often incompatible aspirations. Perhaps it would be helpful to remember that God so loved the *world*—not the church. One of the most conspicuous ways in which the church denies its servant-hood is through the widening credibility gap between its members and the poor. Chapter 6 describes the "Collision Courses" which resulted from viewing a quasi-church program through the eyes of the poor. A clergy-initiated neighborhood association dominated by property owners is contrasted with the desire of tenants and low-to-moderate-income families for self-determination. Even though the Lake Avenue Church was caught in the middle of this tension, it provided more urgency for relating the church's social action philosophy to the needs of specific people in a deteriorating neighborhood.

6   Collision Courses

The lower-class subculture of poverty in Brown Square was separated from the more stable working class in the Edgerton Area by Lyell Avenue. The contrast was so great that this main thoroughfare was often humorously referred to as the "Chinese Wall." The main concern of most Italian residents on the *other side of the wall* was to block the spread of blight already threatening their community. The initial efforts of area clergy to organize the total Edgerton Area had included Brown Square. Originally it was hoped that residents on both sides of Lyell Avenue would be able to work together on common goals, thus ignoring the distinctly different needs of each community.

All of the speakers at the E.A.N.A. constituting assembly had favored no particular religious or political philosophy, but instead stressed the common concerns of the neighborhood residents, most of whom were predominantly Italian Catholic Republicans. Local humor had perpetuated the saying that "St. Anthony's was merely a Republican front with services held in the rear."

While Nelson took an active role in the formation of E.A.N.A., Lincoln merely attended organizational meetings and continued a necessary yet still disjointed ministry in Brown Square. The first obvious collision course which he discovered was the conflict between a landlord and his tenants over a rent strike. This case study had more than passing interest because the attorney for the landlord also happened to be the temporary chairman of E.A.N.A. during its formation and the first year of existence. It also illustrates a typical problem often encountered by low-income tenants of substandard housing, namely the absentee landlord.

Challenging the System

During the course of his pastoral ministry in Brown Square,

Lincoln discovered that the tenants of a certain Lyell Avenue residence had complained repeatedly to their landlord about many unsafe and unsanitary conditions in their apartments. Although some paint had been provided by the landlord in addition to minimum plumbing improvements, much attention was needed in order to make the upper two apartments suitable for occupancy. The two apartments on the first floor had not been visited by Lincoln although numerous attempts had been made. Initial contacts with the tenants in the upstairs apartments were made in the first week of December, 1966, following a rat bite received by one of the children living there during the last week of November.

Upon a thorough examination of these apartments, both families were urged to discuss the physical dilapidation of their respective units with their caseworker, to request an official inspection of the units, and to withhold rent if such action seemed appropriate. An early December visit to the premises by the caseworker gave promise that such a request for inspection would be made. The request was repeated by Lincoln in a phone conversation with the caseworker, and he also disclosed to the caseworker that the tenants were now withholding rent. It was mutually agreed that it would be better if this was not done through the Department of Social Services.

With no further word on this matter from the caseworker or the Bureau of Buildings, both tenants were willing and urged to withhold rent payment voluntarily as an effort to bring the seriousness of the situation to the landlord's attention. Not only were there continuing reports of rats on the premises, but an additional list of thirty-nine complaints and grievances had been listed by one of the tenants. The tenants also reported that in the basement the oil tank was leaking and the fuse box was "spitting sparks." A fire of unknown origin in the basement required the fire department's attention on January 23. It was after this incident that the landlord contacted the caseworker in regard to the rent owed him. A complaint was filed by Lincoln on January 24 with the "Compliance Division" of the Rochester Building Bureau.

Although the caseworker had not sanctioned this action of voluntarily withholding rent, she, the tenants, the landlord, a city inspector, and the landlord's attorney agreed that the apartments were not presently fit for human habitation. They also agreed that it was not financially possible to invest in repairing the property and that the lease should be condemned so that the building could be demolished. According to the landlord, *it had always been his intention to remove the building* for the purpose of providing additional parking facilities and/or expanding facilities of his bakery business, which was adjacent to the dilapidated structure. Demolition of the building had been unnecessarily postponed numerous times. The landlord stated to Lincoln on January 24 that in the "light of all the trouble" the building would be removed by April 1, 1967.

Then a new problem complicated the situation. The landlord wanted to evict all tenants by March 1 and demanded that all rent due him be paid in full. However, everyone else felt that, since the structure was now unsuitable, unsafe, and unsanitary for human occupancy, the back rent was not "due."

In discussing this impasse with the tenants, Lincoln helped them to consider several alternatives which he presented more formally to the landlord's attorney. One solution would be to pay the rent. If, however, the house was not removed in one year and/or any units were rented after April, 1967, the Edgerton Area Neighborhood Association would be asked to employ in a very conspicuous manner the most expedient legal procedures so that an immediate halt would be made to such delay in complying with legal codes and neighborhood wishes.

Another possibility would be for both the tenants and the landlord to assume very adamant positions and bring the matter to the attention of the courts. Such action would result in bad publicity for all. It was also recognized that local precedent implied a favorable decision in behalf of the tenants.

The third and most appropriate solution would be the securing of a legal order of eviction and demolition by the landlord which would be executed on April 1, 1967. The Department of Social Welfare would immediately seek adequate relocation for the tenants and *no back rent*—owed perhaps, but certainly not justly due—*would be paid*. However, full reimbursement for all utilities provided would be made, and the balance would be returned to the Department of Social Services. If a "stay" was necessary because of failure to find suitable relocation sites, the full $84 rent payment would be made for as long as necessary.

Unfortunately, the landlord would not reap a fruitful harvest from the initial investment, but then it was a bad investment from the beginning. For this, all concerned were regretful, yet it cannot be overlooked that it had been the tenants and the community who had suffered most, and it was with them that the greater amount of concern should be shown.

At an E.A.N.A. public meeting, Lincoln privately approached the temporary chairman, who was also the landlord's attorney, and threatened to embarrass him openly with a *conflict of interest* accusation. Faced with several hundred mimeographed copies of the case report, the temporary chairman was persuaded to instruct his client to stop harassing the tenants. It was not necessary to distribute this report because his client agreed to accept the third recommendation. The temporary chairman also indicated that he soon would resign his position as temporary chairman in order to run for city council.

The implication of this lengthy case study was that E.A.N.A. was being used by local candidates of the Republican party whose views were synonymous with a large segment of the Edgerton population. It seemed likely that E.A.N.A. would continue to be used and misused by local politicians for their own benefit unless it assumed an uncompromising stand on some issue considered unpopular within the community. The initial year and a half "reconnaissance" which Lincoln had in Brown Square made it clear that the tenants there were on a collision course with the property owners of the Edgerton Area. Consequently, the Brown Square community planned to break its affiliation with the Association in order to plot meaningful and orderly rapid social change.

Although Lincoln was uneasy about the lack of community among the tenants of Brown Square, it is ironical that he became the bond which drew them together. He also helped them to articulate their dissatisfaction with E.A.N.A. In addition to the conflict between a nonpartisan philosophy and the usage of E.A.N.A. as a platform for political aggrandizement, he also helped them to identify two other collision courses: the conflict between self-determination and church control, and the conflict between the promotion of social change and the preservation of property values.

Motivation Behind Mission

The quasi-church sponsorship of E.A.N.A. gave the impression of church control. Although area clergy were justified in initiating the proposal for the Neighborhood Association, it appeared that they themselves were emerging as the community leaders. This was in part due to their accessibility to one another during the week as well as their desire to be considered urban specialists. Nevertheless, it appeared that an unnecessary dependency upon the clergy was developing among concerned laity and that residents not having area church affiliation were being unconsciously excluded from organizational participation.

The Brown Square community felt that the churches would eventually assume the governing control of the organization. If the starting point were self-determination and not church sponsorship, it is likely that there would be disagreements regarding social action policy, priorities, and appropriate involvement in controversial issues. Such conflict would surely lead to a further decline in the level of residential participation in E.A.N.A., which was limited from the beginning.

A much more serious problem was the conflict between the preservation of property values and the promotion of social change. A genuine concern for tenants and/or low-to-moderate-income families was certainly lacking from the objectives of E.A.N.A. which document the self-interest of the general constituency. E.A.N.A.'s constitution put the emphasis on preserving the property values of the neighborhood (Article III, Section Two):

> The purpose of this organization shall be the gathering together of local residents and interested nonresidents to enhance human dignity and promote civic concern for this neighborhood to the end that it may be *preserved* and developed into a meaningful community. In order to accomplish this goal, the specific objectives of the organization include the following:
> 1. To prevent the indiscriminate granting of further zoning variances in this area;
> 2. To prevent further deterioration in housing and business establishments in this area due to improper code and zoning enforcement;
> 3. To promote optimum land use in this area to the end that property rights will be respected to the fullest advantage;
> 4. To assess traffic patterns and review public safety to the end that maximum protection for all residents may be secured;
> 5. To promote the fullest possible use of all existing recreational facilities and to seek further facilities when needed; and
> 6. To promote the best possible education for all residents.

The need for preserving the Edgerton Area was a direct response to the "spreading blight" in Brown Square. The presence of several junkyard operations in Brown Square had been a long-standing menace to the property owners on the other side of Lyell Avenue. In fact, it seemed that Brown Square was included in E.A.N.A.'s geographic boundaries in the first place because of this junkyard issue. The inclusion of Brown Square also had the advantage of bringing St. Patrick's Church into a closer relationship to the emerging ecumenical strategy. Yet neither of these reasons reflected a genuine concern for that community's residents.

Why, it must be asked, would residents not directly affected by junkyards be concerned with them to the degree that their abolition became a central issue? Why would they be so concerned with abandoned autos on vacant lots and streets, unlawful open burning, and unsightly appearance of junkyards, broken curbs, deteriorating housing, and the decrease in property values in a community in which they did not live? Simply put, neighboring property owners labeled the junkyards as the major cause of blight which no longer could be confined to one community, especially since one operator of a scrapyard was purchasing substantial property in their own neighborhood. Brown Square residential property owners identified with their counterparts of the Edgerton Area who were concerned with signs of impending blight in their neighborhoods.

Perhaps even more importantly, it was observed that these *outside* residents would often suggest that the entire Brown Square area should become a redeveloped park for controlled industry, such as light assembly plants. This kind of land use, they felt, would not only eliminate the major threats to their community like junkyard blight and deteriorated housing, but it would also offer new employment opportunities and an increased standard of living to residents of their neighborhoods. It seemed all too apparent that when the junkyard issue was either settled to E.A.N.A.'s satisfaction or regarded as a hopeless cause and subsequently dropped, the property owners who dominated E.A.N.A. would probably discontinue their interest and energies in Brown Square.

Lincoln continued to minister in the Square with a haunting awareness of these collision courses. He became increasingly uncomfortable as a community organizer for E.A.N.A. How could he be expected to use that association's objectives when he felt that their goals were oriented only to the interests of property owners? To be absorbed in the life of a transitional neighborhood and at the same time to be expected to focus energies on the justifiable concerns of the more affluent at the expense of the poor was an impossible ministry to perform.

An unavoidable part of this nation's urban crisis is how to prevent blight and general physical deterioration to our neighborhoods. Certainly the presence of junkyard operations in predominantly residential areas will accelerate any exodus to the suburbs or at least change the residential pattern from property owners to low-income tenants. Not many people want to raise their families on streets which have become foul-smelling, unattractive, and cluttered with heavy trucking.

However, it must be realized that many of Brown Square's structures are over one hundred years old. The narrow streets are bare because the diseased elms have died and have since been removed. Long before the coming of the junkyards, property owners already were moving out of the community. Often they would subdivide their former homes into several apartments which usually attracted younger Italian couples. Proper building care by their landlords was gradually restricted to minimal maintenance. Eventually many of these properties were sold to slumlord corporations which all but ignored structural and utility repairs. Of course, the tenants of such deteriorated housing then became the poor. First, the rural white emigrant and habitual migrant came, and then the already urbanized black, newly arrived Negroes from the South, and finally the Puerto Ricans. The number of poor, black, and Spanish-speaking families living in Brown Square almost perfectly matched the existing inventory of available rental units of insufficient housing. In only a few instances have blacks and Spanish-speaking peoples actually purchased property. In many of these cases new owners seemed to be harassed by the building bureau due to pressures from various Italian property owners who would report the most minute violations. Discriminatory practice by Brown Square's host society was indisputable.

In summary, it can be concluded that although the junkyards accelerated the process of deterioration, Brown Square had begun dying long before their admission into the immediate neighborhood. Soon only the poor, black, and Puerto Rican families with no other alternative would settle in the area. Similarly, it was natural for property owners to be concerned primarily about their own physical investment. It was natural for them eventually to impose the cause of community deterioration on newly arrived neighbors whose only alternatives were to live in communities of a similar predicament. Natural, too, was it for property owners in adjacent communities to confine the line of blight to Brown Square.

What seemed unnatural was to have the churches unconsciously support the derogatory attitudes of its members who again composed the majority of E.A.N.A.'s membership. St. Anthony's recently built structure possessed an incredibly high mortgage, for which members were hardly able to meet interest charges. Since the prevailing sentiment in the parish reflected the attitude, "Don't bite the hand which feeds you," St. Anthony's could not possibly hope to be a viable agent for social change. Both the pastor and assistant pastor, however, were key leaders in the formation of new ecumenical ministries in the Edgerton Area. They often found themselves at odds with the people of their parish on this issue.

The situation was even more discouraging at St. Patrick's Church, which was located in the Brown Square community. Its declining membership was dependent on three sources of income. First, it had to persuade former parishioners who once lived in Brown Square to continue making St. Patrick's their home church. Secondly, it operated a large and lucrative parking lot between the church and Kodak's main office buildings. Thirdly, it successfully sponsored an annual summer carnival, which attracted people throughout Rochester. The main obstacle in preventing St. Patrick's from becoming involved in dynamic urban mission was not economics but the attitude of its priest. The pastor, who resided outside Brown Square, was well read and knowledgeable of urban problems. He believed, however, that his energies and those of St. Patrick's ought to be directed toward Christian education during the "released-time" school program, preparation for confirmation, and traditional pastoral duties.

Whenever asked to become directly involved in community problems, the parish priest continually used the excuse of his *other* responsibilities and his age of sixty years. A noted Catholic Puerto Rican leader who later joined a Pentecostal church once urged him to give attention to the everyday needs of Spanish-speaking people. He responded by having a South American priest on academic sabbatical celebrate masses in Spanish.

A similar kind of parochial isolation could also be found at the Pentecostal church located almost across from St. Patrick's. Although cordial, the pastor declined to minister to the glaring needs of area people. His theological approach prevented him from being overtly concerned with such secular issues. Personally, it seemed that he was also suspicious and defensive of Protestant interest in the welfare of *his people*. Quite often sect and storefront ministries become possessive of their membership to such a degree that self-preservation and assured in-group community literally isolate them from the world.

On the contrary Lake Avenue Church, the closest mainline Protestant congregation to Brown Square, was extremely vocal about the urban crisis, its causes, effects, and possible solutions. Dr. George Hill had served as president of the Rochester Area Council of Churches in 1964. He endured vicious public attack at that time because of his continued persistence that white churches and local denominational bodies should pledge $100,000 to secure controversial Chicago sociologist Saul Alinsky and his Industrial Areas Foundation to assist Rochester's black community in organizing itself. Lake Avenue Church's suburban-oriented congregation had much to risk. Any drastic reduction in membership would have made the payment of a $370,000 renovation fund debt virtually impossible. The steady decline in membership, as noted below, throughout the five-year experiment is attributed more to geographical convenience of membership in suburban churches than to the pastor's stand for racial justice and economic equality. Note the decline of membership and the increase in the general total budget from 1964 through 1970. The increased figures for the benevolence budget from 1965 to 1969 are explained by the supplemental funds supplied by the Home Mission Societies and the Monroe Baptist Association for the experimental project.

Year	Transferred Out	Transferred In	Total Membership	Benevolence Budget	General Budget
1964	97	64	1664	$31,830	$116,300
1965	124	50	1590	36,520	121,400
1966	62	52	1496	33,900	121,400
1967	146	43	1419	35,750	126,504
1968	69	32	1377	37,264	132,774
1969	74	22	1290	34,000	135,415
1970	52	34	1172	31,000	136,200

Were lay persons from the Lake Avenue Church involved? Partially. Many contributed generous offerings of money, and some participated more directly in urban mission at the local level. Still others supported the Alinsky-style black militant organization called FIGHT, the white counterpart called Friends of FIGHT, which later became Metro Act, and various housing projects. It is unfortunate that those participating in scouting, Red Cross, tutoring, and other volunteer service programs were not acknowledged as performing legitimate mission activity at first. Not until several years later was this serious disservice to the laity realized.

Although few members were directly involved in the inner city, the majority of the congregation continued to support its church which advocated such involvement. However, it cannot be denied that the Lake Avenue Church was becoming polarized and fragmented as the ministerial staff and key lay leaders attempted to call the total congregation to more involvement with local inner-city efforts and related political issues. Some parishioners openly professed their disapproval of grass-root strategies, such as protests, rent strikes, disruption of government and agency functions or threats of even more intense militant action. Some withdrew their financial support of the church; a few even withdrew their membership. Basically, however, the church was held together through these early years of the experiment from 1965 to 1967. This stability can be attributed to several factors.

—The commitment of the congregation to the experiment, even if not totally to the mission it advocated, was firmly established because of the time that was taken for careful planning during the preliminary period.

—The reconciling ministry of a staff which itself was not totally in agreement with the church's new professions, affiliations, and involvements, provided a stabilizing influence for many members.

—The laity of the church knew that in no direct way would rapid social change affect their own socioeconomic levels in distant neighborhoods.

—There was also a willingness at least to engage in general dialogue with those who were more knowledgeable of the urban crisis and who held a different appreciation for assertive strategies.

What role the Lake Avenue Church should assume to the deteriorating Brown Square community just a few blocks away remained an ever-present opportunity disguised as an uncomfortable question. Would this be another collision course, or *would the church have the courage to relinquish its control in order to authentically trust the process of self-determination?* The first major challenge for the church coming from the five-year experiment had been identified. Only time would tell whether the church could make its social-action philosophy operational at the personal level of basic human need in Brown Square.

Looking Ahead to Chapter 7

The collision courses which had caused tension between the Edgerton Area Neighborhood Association and the Brown Square community eventually led to a break between these alternate routes to mission. The contrast was between church-dominated ecumenical ministry and indigenous secular mission in which the church plays a supportive role. Lake Avenue Church was caught in the middle between these two routes and tried to maintain ties in both directions. Whereas the ecumenical style of ministry presupposed church control over its mission projects, the indigenous style of ministry called for "Yielding Right of Way" to the poor. Chapter 7 describes this gradual transition in which the Lake Avenue Church was challenged to relate its social-action philosophy to the needs of people within its adjacent deteriorating neighborhood. When it was decided that secular society should be the focus for urban mission, then the church received direction from the very community it hoped to serve.

7   Yielding Right of Way

Upon graduating from the divinity school in May of 1967, Lincoln remained at the Lake Avenue Church as an appointed urban intern of the Home Mission Societies. Although the small stipend made it necessary to acquire a full-time teaching position at an inner-city school, this arrangement made it possible for him to maintain continuity with the five-year experiment. During this third year he became increasingly dissatisfied with his dual role as a free-wheeling "community chaplain" for Brown Square and a loaned community organizer for E.A.N.A. By September of 1967 he decided to regard Brown Square as a separate entity, which in reality it already was.

With the assistance of three seminarians assigned to his supervision from Colgate Rochester/Bexley Hall and St. Bernard's Seminary, he began to stimulate indigenous interest in neighborhood redevelopment. For weeks they knocked on Brown Square's doors to discuss neighborhood issues, such as junkyard code enforcement, property conservation, school discipline, inadequate recreational programs, rodent control, and population changes. Yet weekly "block club" meetings produced only a few vocal property owners and still fewer tenants.

Finally, in early December, a few property owners openly challenged the right of tenants to have any voice in community affairs. Knowing full well that *tenants* was a polite designation for "niggers, spicks, and white trash," Lincoln quietly began mapping a hidden agenda which he thought would call for an eventual confrontation between the host society and all other community residents.

At one neighborhood meeting he suggested that the duly elected Brown Square vice-president of E.A.N.A., an Italian property owner, appoint as recording secretary a white tenant who was the natural mother of a black child. Without discussion the appointment was made, and the meeting hastily adjourned. Apparently no one was yet ready to discuss the covert economic and racial discrimination which existed throughout the community. Each subsequent meeting produced a few more tenants, while the participation of property owners diminished. Although this development was not anticipated, Lincoln cautiously directed that fliers announcing "block club" meetings be delivered to all community residents.

During this same period, Lincoln began to crystallize the dilemma of community organization in the polarized Brown Square community. Should property owners be regarded as the legitimate voice of the community since, after all, they constituted the largest single unit of the population? Why could the humanity and equality of all residents not be achieved without conflict? What would be the form and results of this inherent conflict? Could a coalition be formed among blacks, Puerto Ricans, and poor whites? What were the responsibilities of Edgerton Area churches to the Brown Square community? Would these churches assume their obligation? What right did community organizers have influencing the destiny of the neighborhood? When does Christian ministry stop being intercession or paternalism and start being intrusion and manipulation?

Lincoln had serious doubts as to whether anything could ever be accomplished by manipulation. Although this issue was not resolved, he and the three seminarians decided to give more attention to the needs of the poor than to the fears of the property owners. The reasoning for this decision was partly based on the simple recognition that property deterioration would steadily continue, thus increasing the inventory of available housing for low-income families. The immediate future of the community belonged to the poor.

While continuing to serve as "community chaplain," Lincoln carefully selected several welfare recipients from each street to serve as temporary block captains. The basis for these selections was not their ability to articulate problems and suggest strategies, as might be expected. On the contrary, with the exception of Jenette Valdez, who was destined to become the community's central figure, none of the dozen or so community leaders were issue oriented. They were chosen because they exemplified multi-problems which were representative of the community's poor, their residential site within Brown Square, and their potential to develop into acknowledged neighborhood spokesmen. Unconsciously consideration was also given to their unquestioned loyalty to the "chaplain" who had helped them in their greatest hours of need. By mid-January of 1968, the Brown Square vice-president of E.A.N.A. was the only property owner attending weekly community meetings.

Because the magnitude and intensity of existential concerns varied among these community leaders, it was impossible to isolate a particular problem as the central issue mandating wide community support. A few wanted the group to be a task force for improving public education. Some thought a rodent control program should be the priority of all residents. Others emphasized better housing, a legal assistance program, medical needs, and home economic classes. From pure exhaustion and exasperation someone said that the goal should be nothing less than "total community renewal." Immediately, everyone responded positively to the idea of embracing all the problems as one, namely poverty. The thought of developing long-range community planning and an efficient local system for providing various social services was certainly challenging.

For a considerable time Lincoln had been concerned that Lake Avenue Church laity had only a few opportunities to be directly involved with urban mission. It seemed to many area residents that the suburban-oriented congregation was merely paying most of the expenses for church-sponsored ecumenical programs in the same way that it had previously been accustomed to supporting generously foreign missions. The additional challenge of relating selected nonresident laity to Brown Square's emerging quest for total community renewal could not be ignored. Lincoln responded by working on a proposal that called for the Lake Avenue Church to sponsor a complete neighborhood center as a means to deal with the problems of the poor.

Mobilizing New Resources

Through three Roman Catholic lay women on the staff of NIP '67 the Lake Avenue Church discovered another ally in its quest for new forms of urban mission. It was a nonterritorial Catholic group called the Community of the Servant of God. The members of this *underground church,* as it was often termed, were laity who believed that traditional Catholic parish structure fostered geographic isolationism and prevented cross-cultural dialogue. In an attempt to break away from such parochialism, thirty discontented families left several suburban parishes in search of personal renewal through service to others. Together they and their *elected pastor,* an ordained Catholic priest who simultaneously continued serving a Rochester parish, gathered weekly for experiential worship, dialogue homilies, and the celebration of the Eucharist as a family meal. Although some members were related to Catholic sponsored inner-city projects, most of the Community members were not involved in any form of urban mission. They, like Lake Avenue Church, were looking for direction.

Lincoln began discussing with both congregations the possibility of joint ecumenical action in Brown Square. What would be the relationship between these two similar yet different Christian bodies? How would this new partnership affect the waning ecumenical relationships among churches in the Edgerton Area? How would St. Anthony's and St. Patrick's respond to the presence of the Servant of God Community which had been labeled heretical by many priests and diocesan officials? What would be the response of the church-dominated E.A.N.A. if Lake Avenue Church's concentration shifted from their blue-collar neighborhood on the north to the increasing poverty just a few blocks to the south? How receptive would Brown Square residents be to nonresidential participation in community affairs? Answers to these questions could come only by discussing the issues with neighborhood residents.

Lincoln approached Jenette Valdez, an exceedingly intelligent and articulate young mother who had long been a resident of Brown Square. Together they discussed the problems of the community, its aspirations, and the need for some expertise if its goals would ever be realized. It was decided that other community residents would be similarly approached and that she would host an evening for residents and nonresidents to meet each other. In turn, he would invite specific laity to attend this cross-cultural experience as an introduction to the community. He would also revise and refine the earlier neighborhood center proposal.

The earlier proposal had requested that funds be used to acquire a building and sponsor various social services, such as home economic classes, a diagnostic clinic, adult education, and a teen canteen. The staff was to include a full-time director, several seminary students, and laity from Edgerton Area churches. The program was to be called WEDGE, referring to an industrial tool which would be used as a symbol to lift up people. Without question it called for a typical settlement house approach for community ministry. Excerpts of that proposal illustrate the kind of foundation upon which a new community development corporation would subsequently be built.

> When a church seeks to minister effectively to a community, it is imperative that in some way it become inherently visible to and identified with those whom it aspires to serve. If this is true, then it obviously signifies an immediate, necessary, and logical extension of local urban mission into the Brown Square community. Our knowledge and love of God coupled with our desire to serve him by ministering to the least of our neighbors summon our physical condescending into this inner-city neighborhood. The biblical and theological roots for this particular form of Christian presence are found in the Incarnation with its mandate for men to reciprocate demonstrative love through participation in the process of intercession.
>
> WEDGE is to be more than headquarters for a social service and recreational program, just as it is to be more than an ecclesiastical derivative to which people can relate or from which a ministry can be performed.
>
> WEDGE is to be an exemplification of Christian presence; a concept that personal and community renewal can be initiated with Christian resources by relating to indigenous people as a means to assist them in confronting their problems; an expression of Christian witness and discipleship as it figuratively takes the empty cross as the appropriate catalytic tool to pry loose trapped human resources from the forces of poverty and disease.
>
> WEDGE has been designed to discover, expose, and encounter the social and spiritual needs of people in the Brown Square community. It will formulate its motives (ends and means) as perceived by the poor people of this community.

To say the least, this proposal was extremely paternalistic, although this limitation was not realized when it was written and presented to the Lake Avenue Church in the winter of 1966-1967. The church's original reluctance to accept the proposal pleased several area clergy, for without Lake Avenue Church's endorsement Lincoln was prevented from presenting the proposal before the local planning unit of the Northwest Ecumenical Ministry. Also, the Edgerton Area clergy could again say that Lake Avenue Church's commitment to the urban crisis was mere rhetoric.

Affirming Indigenous Leadership

A year later in the winter of 1967-1968 Lincoln was determined that the church's previous reluctance to respond to the needs of Brown Square would not recur. Brown Square could no longer be ignored by those who had the responsibility and resources to give assistance. A new approach had to be devised which would bring key lay persons from interested church groups into direct contact with this deteriorating neighborhood. On Valentine's Day of 1968 fifteen residents and an equal number of laity from the Lake Avenue Church and the Servant of God Community gathered in Brown Square to meet one another and to discuss neighborhood problems. The historic importance of this get-together for the future of all concerned is described by Jenette Valdez, whose living room was used for the informal meeting.

It was in December of 1968 that the "community chaplain" told us how he had been interpreting the needs of our community to two nonresident church groups: Lake Avenue Baptist Church and the Community of the Servant of God. We were told that these nonresidents wished to assist us on our terms. "Yea, I bet" was my thought; some even said it. Sure we were desperate but not to the extent where we were going to accept meddlers in our affairs, not to the extent where we wanted things done for us without our consent. No, we were not about to have the church control us for their name's sake. We were assured this would not happen. Okay, let's meet them.

Over the next few weeks a few of us met with them in their homes. We discussed our families, ourselves, and our community. So far, so good. Then on Valentine's Day (February 14, 1968) a love story between a community and the church really began. Thirty selected representatives from the Lake Avenue Church, the Servant of God Community, and our neighborhood met in my living room. *By God, they were listening.* It was evident that the church had learned to take a supportive role in mission, that they were endorsing self-determination, that they were coming to us to be used.

Meanwhile Lincoln was in Chicago attending a church conference on urban mission. During the Chicago conference he came across a paper written by Dr. Jitsuo Morikawa entitled "Ministry of the Laity." There he found articulated a philosophy for urban ministry which had already been verified by his experience. Dr. Morikawa said that the laity cannot be limited to mean just Christians. The people of God include those who hold different definitions of religion as well as those who have rejected all concepts. Christianity is merely one alternative in a pluralistic world. People in every arena of life must have the right to participate in the planning of their destiny. Then Lincoln read something which had never occurred to him before, namely the possessive tendency of the church throughout history to control the projects which it sponsors:

> After all we are a servant church of the Servant Lord and we will settle for a modest colonialism as over against a rapacious imperialism of our forefathers, and be content in establishing our little political Vaticans over which we have control. Since we can't control the whole face of the metropolis, we will manage one part of it—*those projects we sponsor, those ministries we manage, and those programs we finance.* Let us come to terms that no matter how significant, church-sponsored projects are of such meager scale in contrast to the massive character of human need, that we have no right to think of them more highly than we ought to think nor exaggerate their importance or uniqueness in contrast to secular institutions and projects. . . .
>
> If we want the whole world to claim their rightful legacy of God's good gifts, *the secular institutions must be utilized as the major medium of the ministry.*
>
> By insisting that human needs be met by church rather than by the most appropriate agencies and means, it has frequently become a road block toward the maximization of the possibilities of ministry to the whole human community.[1]

Lincoln returned to Rochester with an entirely different perspective of Lake Avenue Church's role in urban mission, especially its role in Brown Square. Fearing he could not quickly convert laity to this new thinking about the *secular control of mission,* he decided to help the community give direction to the church. Having already established the Ecumenical WEDGE Committee, his role in the process of assuring community independence (without jeopardizing needed assistance from local churches) was destined to become confusing and frustrating for everyone.

[1] Jitsuo Morikawa, "Ministry of the Laity" (Valley Forge, Pa.: Department of Evangelism, American Baptist Home Mission Societies, October, 1967), pp. 3-4 (Italics added).

When this new secularized theology of mission was first explained to Nelson, his resistance had been accurately anticipated: "Neither the Edgerton Area clergy nor the broader Northwest Ecumenical Ministry would approve such an idea. If the Lake Avenue Church assisted in the perpetuation of this form of ministry, it would be labeled as a unilateral movement and could severely jeopardize area ecumenism. Brown Square would find itself completely isolated from its most needed and logical sources of assistance." Never did he take issue with the argument, but only with its implications upon existing ecumenical programs which were not "grass-root" oriented.

The more Nelson talked, the more he heard his own words come back to him: "We are on the verge of ecclesiastical ecumenia at the expense of Christian servanthood." At the end of several long and angry sessions, Nelson eventually became committed to this alternate route of mission. He also assumed the responsibility for interpreting it to Dr. George Hill. His resistance was identical to Nelson's until a parallel was drawn. Only a few years ago while serving as president of the Rochester Area Council of Churches, Dr. Hill had successfully taken the initiative to stimulate a metropolitan call for white churches to raise $100,000 needed to acquire Chicago's controversial sociologist, Saul Alinsky, to help blacks develop their own power base. No more needed to be said. Ecumenism at the expense of indigenous secular mission was paternalistic, egocentric, and contradictory to the purpose of the church, which was called to serve the world, not itself.

By the spring of 1968 community residents and suburban laity began meeting together regularly. The long tedious process of developing a viable force for social change had begun. Throughout this process Jenette Valdez emerged as the authorized voice for the poor, a development which angered the Brown Square vice-president of E.A.N.A. The implications were clear. WEDGE, without excluding property owners, would address itself primarily to the concerns of the poor.

Several other developments occurred almost simultaneously. First, tenant block captains attended a public meeting on March 10, 1968, of the Edgerton Area Neighborhood Association, which claimed the Brown Square community as part of its terrain. Speaking one after another, blacks, Puerto Ricans, and poor whites calmly addressed the audience of fifty. They told of their plights, their efforts to develop a poor people's organization which wished to be affiliated with E.A.N.A. while maintaining its own autonomy. Their request for the Neighborhood Association's endorsement was obviously a collision course. Yet their listeners were polite and noticeably quiet. Some applauded. Others murmured. Most remained silent. After a few general questions from the floor, the vote was taken and WEDGE received its first official endorsement. In reality, Brown Square now had two community organizations and one of them, WEDGE, had been authorized by the other.

A second major development followed immediately. Lincoln and his staff of three seminarians urged tenant leaders to hold a mass community meeting to discuss the city's proposed General Neighborhood Renewal Plan. Tenants were reluctant for two interrelated reasons. Firstly, the plan was the concern of property owners, not tenants. Secondly, since community elections were never held, it was conceivable that block captains would be challenged and unseated by property owners. An argument that property acquisition more directly affected tenants than landlords was quickly presented and accepted. However, the issue of authentic neighborhood representation had to be tested.

Fliers and newspaper articles announced the meeting time and place. Suburbanites working with the development of WEDGE who expressed interest in attending the meeting were asked not to come. Some became very angry and demanded reasons for their exclusion from the meeting but were simply told that they would not be welcomed at this meeting which did not concern them. After many accusations and counter-accusations about mistrust and secret meetings, Lincoln intervened. For the first time nonresident laity were told that their role was to assist in developing strategies to meet needs defined solely by the indigenous and to use their influence to cut through bureaucratic red tape or acquire funds when asked. They were to accept their supportive role without question and to seek additional opportunities to neutralize outside opposition to the efforts of the poor whenever possible. This is exactly how the relationships would have to be, how their mission would have to be performed—at least for the present.

As three hundred residential property owners, absentee landlords, businessmen, and a scattering of tenants gathered in the basement of St. Patrick's Church, block captains quietly watched. The seminarians urged tenant leaders to circulate and talk with people whom they knew all too well. Others passed out copies of the proposed renewal plan and a single flier which contained two items: a paragraph explaining WEDGE with check boxes to express approval or disapproval and a proposal to endorse present block captains until community elections could be held later in the year.

The first order of business was a presentation of the city's renewal plan application to Washington and the amount of property acquisition implied. Strong opposition was raised. Then a Democratic city councilman sprang to the floor, pointed to the tenants, and exclaimed to the crowd: "Don't let these people tell you what is going to happen to this neighborhood." Complete pandemonium broke out. Jenette Valdez attempted to gain control of the floor but was shouted down with accusations that tenants had been meeting with the city without the knowledge of property owners.

Lincoln slowly walked from the back of the room to the stage. An elderly Italian woman called to him and asked if she could speak. The crowd calmed as she began. Obviously she was known and respected by most of the people there. She introduced herself as a resident of Brown Square from birth. Then she said: "This is the city's plan; tenants are merely disclosing it." She told of receiving notices of all meetings and pointed throughout the room to those who she knew had also received these announcements. She went on to suggest that the "block club" meetings were not attended by property owners because the concerns of tenants were always thought to be vastly different from those who owned homes. Now, she continued, was the time for a coalition. Several other property owners agreed. The group was split. After several overheated exchanges Lincoln, Jenette Valdez, and a Republican county legislator offered a solution. Present block captains would remain in their current positions to develop the tenant-oriented WEDGE organization while a Citizens' Committee for Urban Renewal of nine members would be formed to develop alternatives to the city's initial neighborhood renewal plan. Each group—resident home-owners, small businessmen, and tenants—would have three elected representatives who together would make up this committee. A nominating committee was made up from volunteers, the WEDGE position statements were check-marked, and then the meeting was adjourned.

While preparing to straighten chairs and lock the building, the president of E.A.N.A. approached the tenants. Together they counted the ballots. Overwhelmingly the property owners signed to indicate their approval of the WEDGE organization—which would have continued regardless of the vote—and, more importantly, endorsed the present block captains. In summary, everyone knew E.A.N.A.'s superficial presence in Brown Square was being replaced by the proposed neighborhood development Citizen's Committee and WEDGE. A suggestion was later made by E.A.N.A. and subsequently followed: WEDGE should disaffiliate itself with the larger organization and become autonomous. In addition to all else which happened, Jenette Valdez had emerged as the poor people's authorized voice in Brown Square.

Soon afterward tenant leaders and suburban-based laity together completed the WEDGE constitution with these stated purposes:

1. To encourage the people of the Brown Square community and nonresidential supporters to improve the life of the poor.
2. To stimulate and develop indigenous leadership, especially among the poor.
3. To work cooperatively with property owners and businessmen as they are represented through the Citizens' Committee for Urban Renewal.
4. To preserve substantial acreage in the Brown Square area for residential land use and compatible commercial structures and activities.
5. To initiate general neighborhood planning for total redevelopment so as (a) to formulate a working Urban Renewal Plan which will foster optimum land use, (b) to promote a fully integrated neighborhood across economic, cultural, and racial lines, (c) to be in agreement with city needs and community concerns.
6. To rehabilitate existing structures when feasible.
7. To encourage and/or cosponsor construction of nonprofit housing for the aged and low- to moderate-income families.
8. To provide through neighborhood facilities appropriate social services deemed necessary by the Brown Square community.

The board was composed of five tenant block captains, a

property owner who was the former Brown Square vice-president of E.A.N.A. and currently a liaison between both organizations, another property owner authorized to represent St. Patrick's, and two representatives each from the Community of the Servant of God and Lake Avenue Church. Although the church was very much present, the community was in actual control of the organization. Application for incorporation as a nonprofit corporation was sent to the state capitol in Albany and granted (as was tax exemption) several months later.

Being new to organization, administration, and program development, the resident board members requested that a layman from Lake Avenue Church serve as convenor of the board, a nonauthoritative position. Similarly, a forty-year-old suburban Catholic layman not affiliated with the Community of the Servant of God and whose easy manner was liked by residents was named interim director. The tasks of broadening the grass-root base, developing indigenous leadership, planning and implementing programs were assumed enthusiastically.

Problems related to impending church domination, however, were not over yet. The Northwest Ecumenical Ministry was trying to dictate some control over WEDGE by blocking Lake Avenue Church participation with that grass-root organization. NEM feared that the Lake Avenue Church would become so absorbed with WEDGE interests that other ecumenical programs would be jeopardized. Lake Avenue Church was reminded that it had covenanted with all area churches not to initiate or fund new ecumenical programs without prior approval of NEM, which had the authority to set all community priorities for the northwest sector.

Dr. George Hill was in a precarious position. Lake Avenue Church had to join NEM or be termed unilateral. He realized that NEM desperately needed substantial funding from the Lake Avenue Church in order to continue various ecumenical programs, especially for youth and children. He also knew that WEDGE was the most appropriate means by which the church could serve the poor of Brown Square. After considerable consultation, the church disclosed its position.

Lake Avenue Church was committed to assist WEDGE, which was acknowledged as a secular organization, not an ecumenical program. "To do otherwise," Dr. Hill said, "would be to deny an opportunity of responsible Christian servanthood. This church is committed to ecumenical ventures and will join NEM if allowed to do so. Any conflict existing between WEDGE and NEM obviously stems from the insecurity of institutionalized religion which has long ignored the quest for self-determination by some of God's people. WEDGE is a channel for equality and reconciliation." NEM said no more until several months later. At this time WEDGE was seeking a facility for neighborhood service programs. One of the options was to utilize St. Patrick's Church for this purpose. Several letters were sent to Bishop Sheen requesting a meeting with him to discuss the matter. When these letters were not answered, WEDGE alerted local ecumenical structures. NEM responded by writing a letter to the Vicar for Urban Ministry. The vicar's reply was encouraging. In the summer of 1968 Bishop Sheen had given a well-publicized sermon in Plattsburg, New York, in which he encouraged churches with minimal parish life to develop maximum use of their property throughout the week by hosting medical clinics, home economic classes, educational and vocational training programs, consumer consultation, cinemas, and other needed neighborhood services. However, despite encouragement from NEM, approval by the Vicar for Urban Ministry, and the Bishop's own stand in this previous sermon, Sheen rejected WEDGE's proposal to utilize St. Patrick's Church for neighborhood service programs. Whether it is a charismatic figure such as Bishop Sheen or some Protestant minister, too often the norm of clergy and church is to preserve their position and property at the cost of mission.

In May of 1968, Brown Square residents learned that Lincoln would soon complete his urban internship. With the backing of her people, Jenette Valdez told the Lake Avenue Church that he was still needed to help develop WEDGE and teach nonresidents their appropriate supportive roles. Dr. Hill and Nelson quickly developed a proposal calling for the church and the American Baptist Home Mission Societies to share equally the expenses in sponsoring Lincoln as a full-time "community chaplain" for the next year. Upon the proposal's approval, Lincoln thanked Jenette Valdez for her participation only to hear her say: "WEDGE, not the church, will tell you when your work is done in Brown Square."

By this time, WEDGE was concentrating on the existential needs of its people. Several projects were operated from private homes and later from a burned-out storefront. Distribution of government-issued surplus foods, a used clothing depot, social services, such as legal assistance and home economics, and recreational programs were supervised by community residents. Approximately thirty nonresident laity were related to these programs and "The Action Groups" (called TAG's) sponsoring them, which were chaired by community residents.

By September of 1968 Jenette Valdez became the executive director of WEDGE. She more than anybody else recognized the necessity to acquire substantial funds if the organization was to meet the needs of Brown Square's poor effectively and become a dynamic force for rapid social change. Proposals were written, sent to various foundations in New York City, and followed with personal visits. In almost every instance a negative response was followed with one question: "Has WEDGE tried Rochester industries?" So crucial was the need for funding that the resident board members decided that the Eastman Kodak Company had to be successfully approached for funds. Everyone believed this to be an almost impossible task. Kodak still remembered its nationally publicized conflict with the FIGHT organization over the number of blacks it employed.[2] If Kodak was to become directly involved with a grass-roots organization, it would make sure this time that it would not become the scapegoat for all other local industries.

Nonresident WEDGE board members, three of whom were employed by Kodak, showed great resistance. The residents knew that they had enough voting strength to approve this strategy, but what would it mean to divide the board? Unanimity was sought. After an intense discussion, the vote was taken and all were in favor of approaching Kodak but one, who chose to abstain.

The elected convenor of the board, a nonresident employed by Kodak, asked if WEDGE would be willing to have him serve as the liaison between the organization and Kodak. This time the residents resisted but only briefly. The proposal was written and submitted with an emphasis that Kodak's existence in the community made its responsibility for assisting WEDGE unavoidable. Xerox, located outside Brown Square, was also approached as an incentive for Kodak to respond favorably.

[2] Prakash Sethi, *Business Corporations and the Black Man* (San Francisco: Chandler Publishing Company, 1970), presents a helpful theory of social systems and the role of business which serves as a framework for the Kodak-FIGHT controversy.

Months went by as corporate and public relations executives of both companies tried to reach a decision. Finally Kodak said it would provide seed money for WEDGE to purchase a building to be used *if* funds for necessary structural renovation could be acquired from another source. Xerox waited and then too responded favorably. Although the total amount of both grants was less than $12,000, this news was like adrenalin to WEDGE, a much needed encouragement to continue on its course of self-determination.

Two of the key persons working behind the scenes in the negotiations with Kodak were the first two convenors of the WEDGE Board of Directors. Both were members of the Lake Avenue Church who found that their involvement in Brown Square was more meaningful than any previous church activity. Listen to the first WEDGE convenor describe the change that this experience brought to his life:

I grew up in the South in a small town which was 75 percent Negro and 25 percent white. When I was a boy, I got in a fight with a Negro girl, and she beat me up. In the midst of tension I called her a "dirty black Nigger." Later that evening my father looked me in the eye and said: "Whatever you do, don't forget the dignity of other people, even if you don't understand them." I've never forgotten that statement. When the riots erupted in our city a few years ago, I was horrified, and I didn't understand why they happened. Our pastor fought for the right of the black community to have a part in the decision-making process of our city, but I resisted him all the way and became disillusioned with the mass community organization which emerged. I haven't been a full supporter of our welfare program, feeling that money was being given to people who didn't want to work. I wanted to help, but I didn't know how.

Then our church started talking about renewal and started experimenting with new forms of community ministry. I ended up as a nonresident member on the Board of Directors of a new community development corporation in the inner-city neighborhood near our church. My contribution as a nonresident is not to run the organization, even though I was elected as the first convenor of the board. The initiative has to come from the residents themselves (blacks, poor whites, Spanish-speaking, and Italians). Perhaps the day will come when the supportive role of nonresidents will not be needed, except for specific jobs which can be assigned. We can put the residents in touch with bankers, industry, lawyers, and others who want to help but don't know how. I am essentially conservative by nature. I want to get as many things done as possible without conflict. At times I have been wrong, but we have been building at a slow and steady pace on a foundation that is rooted in the inner-city neighborhood.

The reaction of Jenette Valdez to the help of nonresidents describes the variety of ways in which Lake Avenue Church members were getting a new exposure to urban mission:

These new friends made available for us a professional urban consultant who has given us valuable direction in planning. They have assisted us in penetrating industry to support our plans. They are helping us establish political backing. Overshadowing all of this, however, is their willing presence in our community and their availability to us at all times: psychiatric consultation at 1 A.M.; medical information at 11:30 P.M.; temporary placement for a youthful offender and subsequent employment; bail money; visitors to those of our community who are in penal and medical institutions; work crews to fix up an apartment; and a cup of coffee in their homes or ours while we talk things over or just relax.

Yes, I've got a different view of the church now. I worship regularly on Sunday morning at the Lake Avenue Church and receive mass in the evening with the Servant of God Community. I can't really say what happened within the church the last year or so, but I'm sure Brown Square is helping the church to see that what it called mission is a liberating force which encourages others to lead while the church stays in the background. Where is the church now? Everywhere at all times ready to help, to get dirty, to get strength, to get involved, to stoop and to pick up.

The first annual "Recognition Night" for WEDGE was held at the Lake Avenue Church on January 3, 1969. Over 120 persons gathered to honor the residents and nonresidents who had made significant contributions to the organization during its first year of existence. Following dinner, an amateur film about WEDGE was shown, and Dr. Harvey A. Everett of the American Baptist Home Mission Societies gave a keynote address. He praised WEDGE for its trail-blazing role as a unique group which was unlike any other to his knowledge across the country. Awards were given to local residents and nonresidents who had formed three action groups to respond creatively to the needs of children for quality education, of youth for recreation, and of adults for social services. The suburban nonresidents were adding their skills to the process in a supportive role. The informality of the dinner, the spontaneity of the singing, the stimulation of the movie, and the personal satisfaction from the awards provided an environment of hope about the future of the church and its nearby inner-city neighborhood. Cutting across boundaries of race, color, and economic status, everyone experienced a sense of fulfillment because a dream was in the process of becoming a reality.

Since the winter of 1969 WEDGE has accomplished many things. It held community elections as promised, intensified its social service and legal assistance programs, developed a weekly diagnostic clinic, produced a twenty-minute community-awareness synchronized sound slide show, and established a youth drop-in center. It also sponsored various community events, such as an inner-city carnival, an art festival, and activities for younger children.

More than programs, however, it has developed a sense of community among Brown Square's poor, several property owners, and numerous suburban laity of the Lake Avenue Church and the Servant of God Community. Nonresident assistance is no longer as extensive as when WEDGE first began. These outsiders simply are not needed as much now with the development of several strong residential leaders. Expertise once only possessed by middle-class church laity now belongs to Brown Square. This is clearly seen in WEDGE's Committee for Neighborhood Development which has assumed the function of the defunct Citizens' Committee for Urban Renewal. This new committee is negotiating for the construction of low-income housing and a new recreational park without any assistance from nonresidents. Presently WEDGE's emphasis with nonresidents is on the raising of additional funds and the cultivation of interpersonal relationships across cultural, socioeconomic, and geographic lines.

Because WEDGE's board is community controlled and its staff is entirely composed of paraprofessionals, some say this little-known effort in Rochester should be regarded as a future model for new neighborhood facilities and existing settlement houses. Such a statement is premature, for WEDGE has its share of internal problems, most of which are related to a still inexperienced staff, administrative inefficiencies, and the continuing time-consuming search for additional funds.

One thing, however, is certain. Without Lake Avenue Church's non-doctrinal ministry through several committed and talented laity, WEDGE would never have been more than merely an idea. Without Lake Avenue Church's unconditional commitment to enable the indigenous to perform professional responsibilities, WEDGE would have become a typical church-controlled neighborhood service center. Without Lake Avenue Church's acknowledgement that secular society is the church's greatest natural resource, WEDGE's quest for industrial and governmental grants might very well have been in vain. And, on the other hand, without WEDGE's patience and persistence, Lake Avenue Church would not have experienced the mandate for this alternate route to urban mission. Thanks to WEDGE, the church was yielding right of way to the poor in order to learn the direction of its ministry. Truly the value which came to the church from affirming indigenous leadership was an unanticipated side of mission.

Looking Ahead to Chapter 8

An automobile that travels beyond the range of its fuel supply will eventually come to a standstill. As the laity of the Lake Avenue Church became more involved in mission, there was also a heightened awareness of the need for spiritual "Refueling." The challenge of urban mission caused some church members to discover new levels of commitment to Christ and new freedom in sharing their faith with others. Whereas renewal was thought of initially as a synonym for mission, it gradually came to mean both the outreach *and* nurture of the congregation.

Refueling

The starting point of the five-year experiment at Lake Avenue Church was the assumption that "the church is renewable." Although not all the implications of this phrase were clear, it was felt that an important part of renewal would be the recovery of relevant urban mission. The early years of the experiment led to the delineation of two alternate routes to urban mission. Route One viewed mission as the development of deliberate church-sponsored projects. If the church is thought of primarily as a gathered community, then mission becomes the dispersion of God's people outward from its center to the broader urban challenge. The first phase of this *centrifugal movement* was aggressive clergy initiation which produced a variety of ecumenical ministries; the second phase was lay leader development which added momentum to this outward thrust. Route Two viewed mission as the enabling of indigenous leadership within the secular structures of society. If the church is thought of primarily as a dispersed community, then mission becomes the utilization of this dispersion as a resource for enabling others to become more fully human. This *centripetal movement* impels both clergy and laity inward to the center of secular institutions.

Gathered Community Extended in Church-Sponsored Projects   Secular Institutions Influenced by Dispersed Community

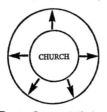 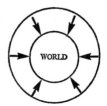

Route One to Mission   Route Two to Mission

Since the church is both a gathered and a dispersed community, it seems that both approaches can be authentic expressions of the gospel.

Yet one troublesome quirk became increasingly apparent about both of these routes—*man* was setting the limits for his involvement and choosing his preference for a strategy of implementation. As lay persons began dropping out of both church-controlled and indigenous-oriented programs, it was realized that a deeper source of support was needed than man could devise. The missing dimension was in the realm of personal faith and commitment to Jesus Christ. Acknowledging his lordship would mean that he would be in control of our lives and would set the limits for our risk-taking in terms of public mission *and* personal relationships. As long as the emphasis was on social action of one form or another, it was possible for man to be in control of the situation and to determine the extent of his risk or involvement. Yet the demand of Christ for obedience also pointed to the need for healing relationships and supportive prayer. Sam Shoemaker put his finger on this deeper level of Christian commitment when he was asked why revival (or renewal) did not come in the way that it was expected. He said: "The clergy themselves lacked the power they might have had if they had even acknowledged *their own need to be further converted.*" [1]

The position of "teaching minister" at Lake Avenue Church was vaguely defined in order to allow for maximum flexibility. It called for a willingness to be experimented upon as well as to develop experimental programs for the church. Perhaps this insistence upon personal involvement was taken lightly at first because it could only be understood in conceptual terms. Initially Nelson thought to himself: "Sure, one would expect to change a few *ideas* about the church but certainly not a basic style of life."

This experiential blind spot was not recognized at the beginning of the experiment because Nelson had not learned how to let lay people minister to him. Whereas many people trusted his judgment about urban mission, others were looking for personal sensitivity and spiritual awareness. They were not being fed by academic concepts or by unusual opportunities for mission involvement.

Although the renewal process had been defined originally as the

[1] Helen Smith Shoemaker, *I Stand by the Door* (Waco, Texas: Word, Incorporated, 1969), p. 106.

task of social change and community improvement, there was also the need for support and nurture in order to affirm church members at the level of personal growth. New ecumenical progams for community ministry were easier to initiate than deeper personal relationships in which the hurts and joys of people could find more adequate expression. It was difficult to communicate this need for healing relationships and personal commitment without sounding judgmental. Although often confused with one-to-one pastoral visitation and hospital calling, the basic need was for a strengthening of the mutual ministry of church members with each other. This concern was not a matter which could be referred to the pastor by saying: "Let George do it." It was a basic question about the life style of the congregation in which a high level of organizational efficiency had been achieved with a minimum of interpersonal involvement and sharing.

Because Nelson was living in the immediate neighborhood near the church, he was viewed by the congregation as an extension of the community ministry which had been inaugurated by previous student ministers. The initial urban dimension of the project set the style for his relationship to the congregation as a visiting specialist in urban affairs. Yet Nelson's involvement in the community heightened his pastoral concern for the spiritual life of the congregation.

The board of Christian mission to which he was assigned as a staff resource person was soon reorganized because several key lay persons also felt the need to diversify the approach to renewal. The former board of missions and the former board of social action had merged into the new board of Christian mission in January of 1966. The "s" in missions was dropped deliberately in order to shift the emphasis from *projects* sponsored by the church to the *purpose* for which the church exists. The need for a more flexible mission structure led to the subdivision of the total board into three working committees, world mission, community ministry, and long-range planning. Whereas the interest of the new board was almost totally absorbed with community ministry, the new pattern of diversification at least called attention to two other areas: the long-standing interest in the church's world mission and the long-overdue reinforcement of the internal life of the congregation.

The third committee on long-range planning started searching for handles to undergird the laity's mutual ministry within the congregation. The two board members on this committee were the key to accelerating the renewal process on the new route of "healing community." Some experimentation with a more personal approach to Bible study followed with the help of resources from Lyman Coleman.[2] Yet these small groups were not composed of key decision makers who could significantly influence the entire congregation.

Starting at the Center

Since the development of this part of the renewal process was in the hands of the laity, the long-range planning committee of the board of Christian mission decided to invite a group of key church leaders to spend a weekend with an outstanding layman from England, Mark Gibbs.[3] The Director of Lay Centers in Europe was scheduled to spend a weekend with representatives from all the major boards of the church as well as the four ministers on the church's professional staff. The neutral setting of a motel on the New York Thruway was chosen purposely to avoid typical churchy patterns. From Friday dinner to late Saturday evening in the fall of 1966 fifteen persons got to know each other in a deeper way. This extended period of interaction opened up another part of the renewal process which was also to go through several phases of development.

No one knew exactly what to expect from the weekend. Yet the end product was a heightened concern for reevaluating the entire educational ministry of the church. The minister of Christian education retired in the summer of 1967. His retirement provided an excellent opportunity for taking a fresh look at the entire educational system before making a staff replacement. Mark Gibbs turned out to be a rather abrasive catalyst who placed a strong emphasis upon education for involvement in the political arena and upon better representation of young people in the governing boards of the church. His most quoted statement, "Little ladies often get killed in a revolution," was an offense to many. His sermon on Sunday morning at the church that same

[2] Lyman Coleman, *Growth by Groups:* A Guide to Renewal Groups in Action (Huntingdon Valley, Pa.: Christian Outreach, Inc., 1965).

[3] Cf. Mark Gibbs and T. Ralph Morton, *God's Frozen People* (Philadelphia: The Westminster Press, 1964). A book for and about Christian laymen.

weekend could be described as shock therapy, and it brought the front line of renewal right into the congregation itself. His deeper involvement with the core leadership group paid off. The result was the postponement of an immediate staff replacement in Christian education for a year until a newly appointed Christian education study group could conduct a thorough research project on the current status and future direction of the church's educational ministry. It was hoped that this study group would come up with some new directions in Christian education which would bring the renewal process to the heart of the congregation.

This decision had a major effect on Nelson's relationship to the congregation since he was asked to shift his main responsibility to Christian education during the interim period of the research project. This opening gave him a new institutional base for testing some of his ideas about the internal life of the congregation. His presence in a more traditional staff role would also tend to legitimize some of his more experimental involvement with the immediate community.

The juxtaposition of the external and internal aspects of church renewal remained in tension throughout the remainder of the five-year experiment. Community ministry received the major amount of publicity during the early years. The emphasis shifted to healing community during the later years. The initial efforts in both areas may be compared to an automobile moving from a secondary road to a major interstate highway. Once the open road was reached, the progress was incredible. The dual-lane highway permitted traffic to proceed on both lanes at the same time. The community ministry traffic moved faster, but the slower and more deliberate traffic which was searching for healing community soon produced results. What started out as an exploratory effort in both cases (E.A.N.A.'s constituting assembly and the Mark Gibbs weekend) was soon followed by more elaborate programs.

Now that Nelson was working specifically within the congregation, he had many opportunities for enabling church members to confront each other at the level of personal faith. The fast moving traffic in community ministry was beginning to slow down because of the need for refueling—for finding meaning at the quiet center of life in response to the claim of Jesus Christ. The second major challenge of the experiment had come into focus: *Could Lake Avenue Church become the kind of healing community which would enable its members to support each other in a variety of mission opportunities that reached out even beyond the immediate community?* The importance of this internal challenge to the congregation will be highlighted by summarizing three tensions which were unavoidable during the early years of the experiment.

First, there was a growing hostility against the tactics being used by FIGHT in its attempt to speak for the black community. The high point of the confrontation with the white establishment was a conflict with Kodak over an agreement to hire six hundred unemployed black workers which was denied by Kodak on December 20, 1966. Notwithstanding the large number of Kodak employees in the congregation, Dr. Hill again took the unpopular side during the controversy on the basis of his understanding of the gospel. Some members expressed their disapproval by abstaining from church attendance; others cut or withheld their pledges; and a few left the church. In spite of these expressions of passive aggression against the position of the pastor, the congregation defended his freedom to preach the gospel as he understood it, even when the members did not like his conclusions.

Second, there was an increasing ambiguity about how far the church should go in cooperating with Roman Catholics. This feeling was expressed openly at the annual meeting in January of 1967, but it was viewed as a minority report. The majority consensus affirmed that urban ministry in the neighborhood would have to be developed in an ecumenical framework if it was to be effective.

Third, there was also extreme sensitivity to changes which had been made in the Sunday morning worship service. In a time of change in every other area of life, the worship service was for many people the main point of continuity with the past. The introduction of a more formal service in the fall of 1964 seemed to reinforce that part of the church's tradition which put a strong emphasis on order, rationality, and objectivity in worship. Some felt that this sophisticated, intellectual approach maintained distance and anonymity among people and left little room for emotion, warmth, and tenderness, which are basic human needs. At a time when a great deal of emotion was being expressed about the tactics of FIGHT and the ecumenical dimension of community ministry, it was essential to find a handle for helping the members of the church respond to each other at a feeling level.

Saturating the Congregation

After considering several alternatives, the long-range planning committee of the board of Christian mission suggested that Faith at Work might be the kind of resource for renewal which would speak to the church's particular situation. The Rev. Lloyd Ogilvie of Bethlehem, Pennsylvania,[4] was the Faith at Work leader chosen to interpret this spontaneous small-group movement to the Lake Avenue Church. On May 9, 1967, he met with the same lay group from the leadership core of the congregation that had spent the informal weekend with Mark Gibbs. Lloyd Ogilvie emphasized the role of small groups in helping his congregation of two thousand members become a healing community. This concern for healing relationship was taken to an all-day church planning conference at Ontario, New York, on May 13. This discussion resulted in the recommendation to the advisory board on June 12 that Lake Avenue Church host a local Faith at Work Conference. The date was set for the weekend of November 30–December 3, 1967. A planning committee was appointed to deal with the bewildering number of details connected with this kind of person-centered event, such as invitations to the visitors, arrangements for lodging and meals, and the selection of hosts and hostesses for many home gatherings.

On several business trips to New York City, Ray Kicklighter became acquainted with Bruce Larson, president of Faith at Work. He was able to alleviate some of the suspicion in the congregation by describing in advance how the conference would work:

> The methodology for a Faith at Work Conference is deceptively simple. A group of laymen are invited to spend a long weekend in the homes of church members. Opportunities are provided for these visitors to relate to as many members of the church as possible during the weekend. These opportunities take the form of businessmen's luncheons, women's kaffee-klatches, and evening home gatherings for adults and teenagers. The hosts for these meetings invite fifteen friends from the congregation in to meet two of the

[4] See Grace Ann Goodman, *Rocking the Ark; Nine Case Studies of Traditional Churches in Process of Change* (Division of Evangelism, Board of National Missions, United Presbyterian Church in the U.S.A., 1968), pp. 159-175; he tells the story of his church, using fictitious names. Cf. Lloyd John Ogilvie, *A Life Full of Surprises* (Nashville: Abingdon Press, 1969).

visitors. The visitors are expected to share their own experience about what it means to be a Christian and how a small-group experience has helped their personal Christian growth. Just a simple series of gatherings of friends to share their hopes, doubts, and concerns for the Christian faith. No big promotion, no posters, no ballyhoo, just a Christian "happening."

The weekend of November 30–December 3, 1967, was just that kind of happening. Bruce Larson was present to coordinate the visiting team and to preach on Sunday morning. Ray Kicklighter summarized the event in a report that he made about the conference:

Twenty-five of the most interesting people you will meet anywhere descended on our church from all over the northeastern United States. They came from other parts of New York, from Ontario, Canada, from Pennsylvania, New Jersey, and Washington, D.C. They represented as diverse a variety of occupations as one could possibly imagine—an engineer, a baker, a businessman, a professor of classical languages, a television actor, a Campfire executive, a social worker, a public utilities executive, a corporation lawyer, a psychologist from Harlem, a clergyman, a redcap porter, and a number of housewives. The one thing they had in common was a sincere love for Jesus Christ and a powerful conviction that this makes a tremendous difference in their lives. More than 250 of our congregation attended one or more of the small-group meetings over the weekend, and perhaps an additional two hundred encountered these visitors during the Sunday worship service and church school.

The reactions to the weekend were as diverse as the backgrounds of the visiting teams. Yet there was a strong feeling that many people in the congregation were uplifted and encouraged by the joyous, winsome spirit of their new Christian friends. Two comments were especially memorable:

The weekend left me with the feeling that we are usually a pretty gloomy bunch. Perhaps we should not take ourselves so seriously.

Before the weekend, the air was full of tension and mistrust among people in our congregation. When the conference was over, I felt that much of the bitterness had been removed.

The members of the congregation were beginning to respond to each other at a feeling level. Much of the hidden and repressed tension came to the surface so that it could be dealt with. The weekend was a source of enrichment for existing small groups and provided a new incentive for expanding this dimension of the church's fellowship.

Another way of viewing the impact of the local Faith at Work Conference is to see it through the eyes of a recently formed small group. The convenor of the group later described the way in which Dr. and Mrs. Douglas Feaver from Bethlehem, Pennsylvania, (who were living in Washington, D.C., at the time) ministered to their new group:

> The five couples in our small group had no previous experience with this kind of personal sharing, except the preliminary exposure that I had in connection with my involvement in a task-oriented mission group. It was assumed at the beginning that some of the group would feel threatened by Bible study, so it seemed more appropriate to begin with a book discussion. We decided to use Keith Miller's *The Taste of New Wine* because his life story would enable us to bounce off of someone else's experience. It has been great for me personally, and the group has done some pretty honest struggling with the issues of faith, prayer, and marriage that are raised in the book.
>
> Three months after our group started, a weekend renewal conference was held at our church which enabled our members to get acquainted with some lay persons from other parts of the country. A professor of classical languages and his wife were invited to meet with our group. We had been fumbling around, reading about a new breed of Christian— a new life—and we really wondered if this was possible for us. The book said so, but we wondered if we somehow had this kind of faith and only needed to work harder at it. We couldn't understand just what Keith Miller was talking about, even though there were familiar elements. It was our out-of-town guests who showed us just what the book was talking about—the committed life. They had experienced the loss of

one of their children but had committed this painful separation into the hands of God. Their personal experience was a model for us. In discussing the book afterward, then we could say: "Remember what our guests said or what they did." Meeting someone first hand was much more compelling than just knowing about a person through a book. Right now our group is struggling to decide whether this new way of life is already present innately in us or whether it is really attainable by focusing more of our attention on it. But the real "sticker" from which we can no longer escape is the uncomfortable question: What is *commitment?*

This was a strange new question to evolve from a group of five couples who were called together originally because of one person's desire to reflect upon the meaning of her involvement with Area Youth Ministry. Because Bible study seemed too intellectual or too remote, the experience of Keith Miller was used as a mirror for reflecting on their own experiences. The guest couple helped to reinforce the content of Keith Miller's book by providing an incarnation of one of its points: "Seeing a *life* with which I could identify did for me what all my 'trying' could not." [5] The small group had accurately distinguished between "knowledge about" Keith Miller and "personal experience with" two guests who demonstrated the reality of Christian commitment. The same difference also applied to their relationship to Christ.

As a result of the Faith at Work Conference the internal life of the congregation had been identified as a long-overdue arena for deeper interpersonal relationships. A by-product of the conference was two related developments which were particularly directed toward new members and maturing members.

The presence of the Rev. B. J. Cannon of Bethlehem, Pennsylvania, for a School of Mission program in February of 1968 alerted the church to an experimental approach to new member orientation that he had developed.[6] "The Inquirer's Group," as he called it, met in the homes of participants for six consecutive weeks and concentrated on helping people get to know each other. Sharing one's spiritual autobiography helped participants to make new

[5] Keith Miller, *The Taste of New Wine* (Waco, Texas: Word, Incorporated, 1965), p. 58.

[6] Cf. Bryan Jay Cannon, *I Give Up God* (Old Tappan, N.J.: Fleming H. Revell Company, 1970).

or renewed commitments to Christ. This approach was tried at Lake Avenue Church during the spring of 1968 with considerable success.

This School of Mission also set in motion a controlled experiment of eight sessions every other week for ten *koinonia* groups which had the option of deciding whether they wanted to continue meeting beyond the initial period. Many maturing church members found a base of support for Christian growth and reflection on mission from these sessions. The new direction was the willingness of some church members to go to other churches as a visiting team in order to share their experiences in church renewal. The first group of thirteen went to Hamilton, Ontario, in March of 1968 for a "Concern for the City Weekend" at the Zion United Church.[7] The second group of five went to Caledonia-Mumford, New York, in December of 1968 for a weekend Faith at Work Conference sponsored by five village churches. As Lake Avenue Church laity took the lead in reporting on what was happening in their lives, they also learned anew that it is in giving that we receive.

The continuing ministry of Faith at Work as a leader development resource in the congregation was felt by sending people to the New York State Regional Faith at Work Conferences which were held each fall near Corning, New York. The way in which this regional conference spoke to the needs of a key church member in the fall of 1968 will illustrate how Faith at Work helped to undergird the church's involvement in mission. The problem which this suburban housewife took to the conference was extreme anxiety about the conflict within a lay staff which was attempting to minister to alienated youth. She was personally disappointed when her leadership role in a task-oriented group was denied and passed on to someone else who was more aggressive. The realization of her basic self-centeredness came to the surface when she was unable to adjust to the new situation. The small group to which she belonged at the Lake Avenue Church dismissed the problem as oversensitivity and thought that her expectations were too high. During the course of a heated discussion at one of these small-group sessions, she said: "Only God can call us to come to

[7] Charles Wilkinson, "Protestant, R. C. Churches Combine to Head Off Violence: Experiments in Brotherhood Stress Listening, Self-Help," *Hamilton Spectator* (April 20, 1968), p. 18.

him; we can't earn a place for ourselves in the kingdom of God."
Yet her negative understanding of self-centeredness detracted from
her sense of worth and stood in the way of hearing God's call.

A new beginning was experienced at the Faith at Work Conference where she announced to another small group that she was
only a "prospective Christian." The verbal responses there had
turned her off. It was the nonverbal caring of several sincere
Christian strangers that helped her to believe that God could love
and accept her as she was. The one whom God chose to call her
was a mailman. When confronted with the problem of self-centeredness, he said: "Perhaps even that aspect of your life has the
possibility of being used by God." A positive response meant that
God could even accept her egocentrism. In the middle of the same
night of confused thoughts, she decided to give her life to God.
The next morning she confirmed this decision with the mailman by
saying: "God, I want to take myself out of the center of my life
and put you there." He asked: "Does that mean you also want
to accept Jesus Christ as your Savior?" She replied: "In blind
faith I accept Jesus Christ as my Savior."

The implications of that decision were being worked out as she
found her place again in the Area Youth Ministry. Her leadership
role was no longer being used as the only hope for "earning her
way into the kingdom of God." Now it could be channeled toward
redefining the goals of the program and developing new forms of
ministry. She had learned that the existence of conflict within herself could be the occasion for a new experience of Christian commitment.

The Rochester group at the same conference held a caucus before leaving and decided to plan a training event for others in
their area who would profit from further emphasis upon "The
Affirming Life." Two weeks after the WEDGE "Recognition
Night," Lake Avenue Church also hosted a small-group workshop
in mid-January of 1969. About 120 persons attended this all-day
session. The purpose of this workshop was to sensitize the participants to the areas of ministry which were within the limits of
their daily experience. There was joyous singing, an inspirational
address, the sharing of personal experiences, and spontaneous
prayer. A time of sharing had been held the night before in order
to prepare the resource team for the conference. Members of the
team and the rest of the conferees came from a 100-mile radius,

providing a good cross section of several denominations and geographical settings. The closing worship service was led by lay
persons who challenged the entire group to use the many routine
experiences of daily life as an arena for living out the Christian
faith. The greatest encouragement came from hearing about the
successes and failures of others who were struggling to be obedient
to Christ in their family, on the job, or in their neighborhood. The
entire day was marked by a sense of joyous celebration. The wide
variety of participants from urban and rural backgrounds left with
a new determination to view all of life as a crucible for growth
toward wholeness of ministry.

Something new happened on that day at the Lake Avenue
Church which cut across the grain of its strong issue-oriented life
style. Lay people from all walks of life and many denominations
were helping each other discover their ordinary gifts for ministry.
A new balance was beginning to emerge between the external and
internal aspects of church renewal. Then it became clear that *renewal is actually "commitment to a process"* [8] *aimed at discovering
wholeness of ministry.* For the Lake Avenue Church that process
was first a renewed commitment to the world and then a renewed
commitment to Christ. Although only about one hundred church
members were engaged in either or both aspects of this search for
new forms of congregational life and mission, significant progress
had been made in both directions. The church had tested its "responsibility" (literally response-ability) to its immediate community and its congregation. In addition to reclaiming essential
values from the past and rethinking accepted patterns of the present, this renewal process also led to the reordering of priorities for
the future. The development of a strategic-planning process for the
entire congregation was a "spin-off" of this tension between the
external and internal aspects of renewal.

The new concern about healing community did not take the
Lake Avenue Church by storm. Although the Faith at Work Conference succeeded in bringing many people together in new groupings, it was several months after the conference before these small
groups began to sense their responsibility for a mutual ministry of

[8] William R. Nelson, "Church Renewal: Commitment to a Process,"
Minister (The Ministers Council of the American Baptist Convention,
Valley Forge, March, 1969), gives a summary statement of the first four
years of the experiment.

support and encouragement to each other. The first route of this internal quest had at least put a new item on the continuing agenda of the congregation—*the need for more emphasis upon the mutual ministry of the laity with each other.*

At the same time the different approaches taken by the professional staff could not be ignored. Each of the three full-time ministers was so different that the Lake Avenue Church actually had a style of ministry for almost everybody. There was a leader for the pietist who liked *Bible exposition,* for the laity who wanted support for living out their faith in the context of *relationships,* and for the social activists who wanted the church to deal with *public issues.*

The varied talents of the professional staff could have projected a comprehensive view of evangelism by which the gospel is proclaimed *(kerygma),* lived *(koinonia),* and demonstrated *(diakonia).*[9] The interaction of proclamation, fellowship, and service constitutes the ingredients for wholeness of Christian ministry. Yet this interaction could only have happened if there had been a genuine desire of all three ministers to share their strengths and weaknesses with each other and their key admirers. Instead, each operated his separate department of the church in polite but "arm's length" distance from the other.

The only hope of developing a real team ministry at the heart of the church had to come from the laity's ministry with the professional staff. The new experience with small groups had caused some lay persons to change their expectation of the clergy from the role of pastor director (organizer, administrator, promoter) to that of lay enabler (resource, equipper, trainer). Therefore, a by-product of the growing expectation for a mutual ministry among the laity themselves was *the development of a new relationship between clergy and laity.* The new expectation for the professional staff may be described as a shift from the "driver's seat" to the resource position of "backseat driving" (see chapter 1). This change was an attempt to reverse the passive "follow-the-leader" pattern of many lay persons and the "one-man-show" orientation

[9] J. C. Hoekendijk, *The Church Inside Out* (Philadelphia: The Westminister Press, 1964), pp. 25-26. Cf. Elizabeth O'Connor, *Journey Inward, Journey Outward* (New York: Harper and Row, Publishers, 1968), for a highly disciplined approach to this quest for wholeness of ministry within the Church of the Saviour in Washington, D. C.

of the ministers. It is one thing to read in the Letter to the Ephesians that the minister's primary job is "to equip God's people for work in his service" (Ephesians 4:12, NEB), and it is something else to do it.

In summary, the external quest for church renewal produced two complementary routes for expressing the service *(diakonia)* dimension of the gospel. These two external routes are described by Rüdiger Reitz as the contrast between *parochial ministry* and *functional mission.*[10] The first external route takes its point of departure from one or more central gathering places from which church members disperse in service to the world. The second external route refers to the way in which dispersed church members meet outside the parish in scattered secular places where those in need live, work, and celebrate. In other words, living out the demand of the gospel for service to others can be accomplished in a geographical setting or a functional setting. The particular opportunities in the northwest sector of Rochester led to the development of an ecumenical ministry in the geographical setting of a larger parish consisting of seventeen churches. The functional approach to secular mission resulted in the formation of a community development corporation to deal with the broad range of human need associated with "poverty structures."

The internal quest for church renewal also produced two complementary routes for a more personal approach to the demands of the gospel for fellowship *(koinonia)* and proclamation *(kerygma).* The first internal route which has just been described consisted of a heightened awareness of the need for *mutual ministry,* both among the laity themselves and between the clergy and laity. The tensions created by the external routes called for a deeper experience of love and reconciliation in the congregation. The new concept which needed embodiment was the hope that the church could become a "healing community." Rather than responding to this need just through passionate pleas from the pulpit, *new forms of congregational life* had to be developed which would give concrete expression to this kind of healing community. This

---

[10] Rüdiger Reitz, *The Church in Experiment* (New York: Abingdon Press, 1969), gives many examples throughout the United States of these two external routes. Although he surveys many renewal experiments, his basic distinction between "parochial ministry" and "functional mission" is verified by the five-year project in Rochester.

second internal route will be described in the next chapter with specific reference to the process of institutional change. The preliminary attempts at long-range planning through the Christian education study committee and the board of Christian mission continued to pay off because of the unrelenting follow-through.

Looking Ahead to Chapter 9

It has been demonstrated that the high-speed traffic on the highway of ecumenical ministry sponsored by the church or secular mission indigenous to the community cannot keep up forever without necessary stops for refueling. During the course of refueling it is also helpful to check the map in order to determine the most appropriate road ahead for reaching the desired destination. In relation to the experiment in church renewal, chapter 9 will show that "Checking the Map" is actually engaging in a process of strategic planning aimed at more fully demonstrating wholeness of ministry to all of God's people. Beginning with the church's educational ministry, the planning process was soon expanded to include the concerns of the entire congregation through the minister's cabinet. The need for healing community was reinforced as the main priority of congregational life. In addition to the continuing emphasis on small groups, this need was responded to more concretely through new forms of experimental worship and of parish organization.

9 Checking the Map

A stop for refueling in the course of a trip is also a good time for checking the map. While actually on the road, it is often difficult to read a map carefully. The best way to avoid unnecessary mistakes en route is to plan ahead the most appropriate route for reaching a desired destination. Few people will take a trip without knowing rather specifically where they are going and how they can get there most conveniently.

If it is agreed that every church should be in a continual process of institutional change aimed at more fully demonstrating wholeness of ministry to all of God's people, then it will also be necessary periodically to check up on the actual steps which have been taken to move closer to this goal. The basic question is: *How can a church build into its institutional life a strategic-planning process which will enable continual renewal to take place?* This continual search must begin with those needs which are immediately discernible and move on to those areas which cannot be foreseen.

At the Lake Avenue Church the planning process began in response to the immediate need for projecting the future goals of Christian education before adding another person to the church's professional staff. The continuing process of setting goals for the entire congregation was given to the minister's cabinet. This dormant group had been accustomed to meeting periodically on call from the senior minister for the purpose of determining the agenda for the advisory board meetings of the congregation. In order to emphasize its new role, the minister's cabinet was reestablished as a long-range planning committee of the church by the advisory board in March of 1968. This committee consisted of the chairmen of official boards, full-time staff, the church moderator, and three members from the church-at-large. Its purpose as recorded by the church clerk was to discuss the "style and purpose of our church life." Because the prevailing mood of experimentation had produced conflicting responses among segments of the congregation, it was necessary to evaluate the most significant options for ministry in the light of past precedents and future possibilities.

The development of such a planning process must find a balance between continuity and change. Continuity provides a grounding in the best of past traditions which make each church distinctive. Change assumes openness to the future in which the congregation is in the continuous process of becoming a more faithful embodiment of the people of God. Change by itself does not mean renewal. Change only becomes renewal when it is aimed at achieving goals which enable the congregation to deepen its commitment to Christ, to one another, and to the world.

Although technically called a "long-range planning" committee, the advisory board actually initiated a "strategic-planning" process. Long-range planning traditionally refers to predicting the future five to ten years in advance and then establishing overall or specific objectives to be reached by an organization at some specific future date. Although some attempts were made initially to follow this pattern, the committee actually followed the pattern of strategic planning which had already been set by the Christian Education Study Committee. Strategic planning is defined by Richard Broholm as "a process by which an organization *continuously* plans for the future by bringing its present assumptions, objectives, and strategies under constant criticism and review in order to facilitate adaptation to future conditions, to make its operations more flexible, and to assure a clear sense of direction." [1] The preliminary step in this direction with respect to Christian education was not an end in itself but a means to the end of challenging the congregation to plan continuously for the style and purpose of its future ministry. Again it is apparent that the process of institutional change is the science of follow-through.

Education for Mission

Changes in the ministerial staff of a church may provide one of the best opportunities for initiating a process of strategic planning. The slowing down of the usual procedure for replacing the director of Christian education at the Lake Avenue Church made

[1] Richard R. Broholm, *Strategic Planning for Church Organizations* (Valley Forge: Judson Press, 1969), p. 32 (Italics added).

it possible to make a thorough study (from March, 1967, to February, 1968) of the church's teaching ministry. The officially appointed Christian Education Study Committee of ten lay persons was to make its report to the church for the purpose of guiding the ministerial selection committee. In other words, the new staff person would be interviewed and called on the basis of his response to the self-conscious educational objectives outlined by the study committee.

The committee assumed from the beginning that "education must become the central thrust of any attempt at renewal of the church" and that "education must be seen in the broader framework of the mission of the church." Its task was facilitated by dividing into three subcommittees in order to deal with ministry to children, youth, and adults. Many evaluation forms were filled out by the board of Christian education, church school teachers, parents and children in the church school program, adult members of the congregation, and the ministerial staff. Key people from secular and religious educational institutions were consulted. Field trips were taken in order to learn from other searching congregations.

The final report affirmed the central role of education in the life of the church and called for the laity to accept the full responsibility for its implementation. Instead of the familiar pattern of calling a director of Christian education, the report recommended the calling of a minister of education who would enable the laity to fulfill their primary responsibility for the church's educational ministry. It also recommended that the major responsibility of the board of Christian education and the new minister would be to initiate and evaluate experimental programs, such as non-graded groupings by interests and family celebrations. It was hoped that more disciplined programs calling for greater involvement and commitment could be developed. Likewise new home-centered programs designed to make family religious training a reality would be explored.

With the help of these recommendations which the ministerial selection committee used for overall direction, the church called the Rev. Claude A. Pullis to join its professional staff in September of 1968 as minister of education. His operating philosophy of education for mission and his specialized interest in experimental worship and family celebrations were directly related to the projections of the study committee. His coming fortunately coincided with the launch of a new denominational curriculum resource (American Baptist Christian Faith and Work Plan) which strongly emphasized experiential learning. The training events connected with this new three-year curriculum series further developed the interest in small groups which had gained considerable momentum from the previous Faith at Work Conference. (The latter small-group movement is interdenominational and has no connection with the Christian Faith and Work Plan.)

Rather than restricting his attention to teaching-learning through the church school, Claude Pullis had a broad interest in education for mission. His availability to the immediate community was formalized by his serving as a resource person for WEDGE's action group dealing with the problems of education in Elementary School #5. Nelson was also able to resume some of his earlier involvement in the community by serving as a resource person for WEDGE's action group dealing with social services. Lincoln continued to work in the background, writing proposals and establishing contact with key people in industry for the purpose of additional funding. The presence of the new minister of education on the church staff was a source of personal support to both Nelson and Lincoln since all three shared in common the role of change agent both within the congregation and the community.

One of the most obvious changes during the fourth year of the experiment largely associated with the special talent of Claude Pullis was experimentation with the Sunday morning worship service. The Christian education study committee had called for more responsibility on the part of lay persons in the church's educational ministry. Since this concern included worship, it was felt that lay persons should participate in the planning for at least a few representative services. It was agreed that each of the church's official boards would appoint a subcommittee to work with the ministerial staff. A schedule was developed so that these five experimental services would be no more frequent than once a month. As an example of this mutual ministry between clergy and laity, one of these worship services will be described in considerable detail.

The experimental worship service planned by the board of Christian mission was aimed at affirming the role of the average members of the church in mission. In a congregation with strong activist tendencies, it was important to keep extending the boundaries of Christian witness beyond the visible core who were involved in new forms of community ministry. The planning committee which decided on this theme then proceeded to develop a design which would give it most adequate expression. The theme would be introduced by rewriting the text of the spiritual "Were You There When They Crucified My Lord?" The emphasis would be on contemporary manifestations of the crucifixion in everyday life, such as the emptiness of the forgotten stranger on the street or the loneliness of a deeply troubled mind. There would be a time for the sharing of prayer concerns from the congregation in order to point out the variety of mission opportunities. The climax would be a trialogue sermon entitled "Where Am I?" by a clergyman and two lay persons. The laity would be chosen as representatives of the two extremes in the congregation: a traditional churchman who mainly chose to implement his concern for mission through church structures and a radical activist who mainly chose to implement his concern for mission through secular structures. The clergyman would enable them both to relate their personal involvements in everyday life which extended their Christian witness beyond their more typical roles. Supplemental material from T. S. Eliot and Kahlil Gibran was added to the liturgy. Five lay persons, a clergyman, a soloist, and a choir led the congregation in this experimental worship service.

A sense of freedom and spontaneity was evident throughout this worship experience even though the order of service followed the same general outline which was regularly used by the congregation. Several points kept recurring both in the formal and informal evaluation following the worship experience.

—It was generally agreed that the process of preparing for the service was the most valuable part of the experience. Members of the planning committee became better acquainted and discovered unknown talents and attitudes which were woven into the final tapestry.

—This special service was aimed at reinforcing the variety of mission opportunities that were available to the average members of the church. It was designed to counterbalance the extensive public interpretation which had been aimed at promoting the more specialized forms of mission to the community. If renewal was to capture the imagination of larger numbers in the congregation, it could not be restricted to the small core group of those who chose to become directly involved in new mission projects. The service was a plea for the unorganized response of individual members to the ordinary occasions in which the gospel could be shared with others through word and deed. The unusually high level of interest in the pulpit-pew dialogue which followed the service was an indication of the number of members who had been personally challenged by the experience.

—The strain upon the planning committee which emerged from the process was an unexpected conflict of musical tastes. In a church that is especially recognized for the high quality of its musical program, there was considerable reserve about the appropriateness of adapting the spiritual "Were You There When They Crucified My Lord?" The conflicting opinions could not be reconciled, and this inconsistency between liturgy and life left the planning committee with a sour taste for months after the event.

In spite of a few rough edges the service was an embodiment of the heightened pastoral concern of Lincoln and Nelson for the average members of the church. By working in the background with the planning committee, they tried to apologize for their initial impatience in wanting to associate with only the few activists who thought as they did.

Institutionalizing the Gains

The gradual unfolding of a process of institutional change was the main contribution of the fifth year of the experiment. An accelerated process of strategic planning made it possible to conserve and institutionalize the gains which had been made during the previous four years. With the coming of Claude Pullis, the minister's cabinet started meeting more regularly in order to clarify the overlapping of job descriptions. Because of his concern about education for mission, his job description was expanded to include some involvement in community ministry. In addition to Dr. Hill's broad pastoral responsibilities and preaching ministry, he was asked to be the church's staff representative on the Northwest Ecumenical Ministry Board. The associate minister was asked to give staff support to the planning of a Parish Zone Plan.

Nelson continued to devote his main attention to supporting the small-group ministry of receptive church members who were being challenged by Bible study, personal sharing, or book discussions.

An added complication came with the impending termination of the five-year experiment when supplemental funds would no longer be available. It was generally assumed that the full-time staff of ministers would be cut back to the normal number of three at the end of the five-year period. Therefore, the advisory board reestablished the minister's cabinet as a long-range planning committee in March of 1968 to consider how the gains made during the experiment could be institutionalized in a more permanent way. This committee consisted of the minister's cabinet plus three members from the church at large. The responsibility for evaluating the experiment was assigned to a smaller committee which reported its findings to the long-range planning committee on June 26, 1969. Excerpts from that report provide an inside view of the renewal process:

> In the Mission to the Community, approaches have been ecumenical, secular, Christian, political, personal, abrasive, warm, assertive, tentative, and selfless. Many have been truly experimental pioneering efforts with no previously charted course. There has been waxing and waning, changing of direction or emphasis, some maturing and some withering. In many areas, only surfaces have been scratched; in others, perhaps solid beachheads have been established. Our finest hours were where we offered ourselves to be used rather than run the show.
>
> What has been the effect on Lake Avenue Baptist Church and its people? Some persons involved indicate that they have enjoyed satisfaction but have experienced no discernible personal spiritual renewal. On the other hand, some report changes which go to the core of their being. Some members not involved feel personally uncomfortable or that the church is misdirecting its resources. A few of these have left the church and more just stay away. Other members, not directly involved, experience a real but vicarious renewal because of the presence of involvement, the conscience and challenge of immediate mission and their moral support of it or concerned reaction to it.
>
> Some of the membership loss and much of the attendance loss over the last four years has been due to the manner in which our efforts toward renewal have been communicated to the membership. We have made these people feel guilty, alienated, or forgotten. In a few cases we couldn't have helped it; in most cases we could have.
>
> If only a small percentage of the membership can paddle a particular canoe, it is the quality of *their* experience which counts and judgments against the non-paddlers should come slowly if at all. One of the real contributions of the small-group approach to renewal has been the

sharing of loads, insights, and experiences without feeling the need to be judgmental of others. It becomes apparent that so often we know not what loads another bears until we offer to share it with him.

It is good that we accept and are accepted by people of other cultures and creeds. It is not good when we imply (however misunderstood) to our own members that *they* cannot be accepted unless they change.

The efforts of the last four years have been a valuable experiment from which much can be learned and some retained. Wholeness of ministry is the goal. Outreach to the community or elsewhere is a part of it, but only a part. Reflection, education, and ministry to each other are equally important.

In an experiment which assumed the necessity of change, this evaluation indicates that versatility became an essential ingredient of the entire process. It is also apparent that the experiment became a threat to the status quo of the congregation. Yet innovations in the area of community ministry rightly needed to be complemented by new forms of mutual ministry within the life of the congregation. The long-range planning committee came to the realization that a new style of mission to the community would only be accepted when it was reinforced by a deeper level of trust among the members of the congregation. Everyone wanted renewal, but few were willing to pay the price of learning to accept one another in love.

Thus, the long-range planning committee members prepared individual statements of their hopes for the Lake Avenue Church during the next five years. By pooling their resources and sharing their insights, this process of strategic planning led to the presentation of a final report on February 9, 1969. Repeated refining of the material had taken place until the desired degree of clarity was attained for this final report. It consisted of assumptions, objectives, strategies, and tactics.

The underlying premises or *assumptions* of the planning process were called the purposes of the Lake Avenue Church:

—To be a fellowship through which God can make himself known to us. (We come to know God through history, through people, through the records of the Bible, and especially through Jesus Christ.)
—To be a fellowship in which we are able to respond with trust and commitment.
—To provide the support necessary for us to live and grow in obedience to God.

—To be a community of love where we bear each other's burdens as a mark of our authenticity.

It may seem that these assumptions are limited rather unnaturally just to the internal life of the congregation. The church's strong stand on public issues was so well known that the committee chose not to reemphasize it here. Instead, they picked up the hope for "a community of love" as a direct response to the anxiety and tension caused by the experiment.

The *objectives* of the planning process were listed as specific goals:

—To be a "healing community" wherein its members find through each other the support and strength they require.

—To recognize that the church is composed of lay and clergy ministers. Each must fulfill the ministry to which he has been called. The context of the Christian ministry is in the world of which "the church" is but one facet.

—To educate its membership for ministry in the variety of settings in which the Christian finds himself.

—To train and orient new and present members as to the meaning and responsibilities of membership in Lake Avenue Baptist Church and the Christian church-at-large.

—To continue our ecumenical involvement.

—To continue our emphasis on mission to our neighborhood, the city, and the world.

—To continue our church's prophetic voice, raising the critical issues of the day, and challenging its members and society at large to the practice of love, justice, and peace.

—To act corporately in response to these issues.

—To provide worship opportunities meaningful to the variety of needs within our congregation.

—To improve communication and interpretation within and between staff, boards, congregation, varying age groups, and the community.

—To establish a means for continuous evaluation and long-range planning resulting in recommendations to appropriate boards for consideration and implementation.

—To promote the spirit and practice of evangelism through being, telling, and doing the gospel.

Although not intentionally listed in order of priority, the internal life of the congregation still received prominent mention at the beginning of the list. The phrase "healing community" was introduced to key members of the church by Lloyd Ogilvie prior to the Faith at Work Conference.

The *strategies* of the planning process consisted of three courses of action for carrying out the objectives related to cabinet-staff relationships, functions of ministry, and staff responsibilities.

—Effective lay-clergy relationships would be assured by recommending that the cabinet meet regularly with the staff for purposes of planning, communication, counseling, and accountability.

—Present programs and job descriptions should be reviewed with respect to the following framework: receiving ministry, training ministry, sending ministry, and supporting ministry.

—Staff responsibilities should be reviewed periodically so that jobs could be reassigned to better handle specific programs.

These strategies document the new aggressive role that lay persons were taking in the church's total ministry. Their ministry with the staff was an important step toward the development of a genuine team ministry among the clergy and between clergy and laity.

The *tactics* of the planning process took the form of four specific steps that required the urgent and concentrated attention of the staff during 1970:

—Immediate and effective implementation of the parish zone concept as a means of developing a "healing community" within our congregation.

—Development of an urban chaplaincy as a component of our mission to the community.

—Development of more effective planning of staff activity in order to achieve the specific goals and to more efficiently implement the programs of the church.

—Improved communication between staff and boards of the church through regular meetings of staff and cabinet.

The new expectation for the ministerial staff of "backseat driving" was affirmed by a concluding statement: "The committee feels that it cannot overemphasize the importance of development of the 'ministry of the laity.' The staff is expected to approach all programs and activities in such a way as to develop increased commitment on the part of the laity."

As Nelson looked back over the five years in Rochester, he realized that God had been preparing him all along for another position. In June of 1970 he became program director for the American Baptist Assembly in Green Lake, Wisconsin. During the five-year experiment he had shifted roles from either a theological or urban specialist to that of a generalist. In both of these previous areas of specialization his adaptability to the total environment was limited. Shifting to the role of generalist made it possible for him to develop some new specialties, both small-group ministry and pastoral administration. This variety of training and experience provided the kind of versatility which was required for the Green Lake position. His interest in church renewal could be utilized as the central concern for a new thrust in program development at the Ameican Baptist Assembly.

The lessons learned about himself and the church did not come easily. They grew out of a few deep and lasting relationships with people who made a difference in his life. The one from whom he learned the most was Ray Kicklighter. This research physicist with the Eastman Kodak Company asked some disturbing questions while reminding the church that the renewal process there was really just beginning:

Can we claim that the church has been renewed, based on the actions of a few dynamic leaders and a few dozen committed participants, or must something significant happen in the life of the congregation at large? In reflecting on this basic question, a number of us concluded that a renewed church is, first and foremost, a church made up of renewed people. This is one of those absurdly obvious truths of which we must continually remind ourselves. The implications are clear. *Renewal is not a goal to be attained but rather a process in which to engage.* Our success may then need to be evaluated, not so much in terms of the activities of the avant-garde but by the degree to which we provide the environment in which nominal Christians can be transformed into truly committed disciples. In short, how can all of us in the church claim the wholeness inherent in the Christian faith? There is a real danger that we may be misled into thinking that because we talk about renewal we are actually achieving it.

Although no one expects the route ahead to be straight and without new detours and collisions, the ultimate destination is much more certain. It may be described as movement toward wholeness of ministry in which an increasing number of God's people will discover for themselves the risk of involvement and the joy of personal growth.

Looking Ahead to Chapter 10

There is a big difference between going out for a rambling drive and setting out for a specific destination. This difference characterizes the changing style of life at the Lake Avenue Church from 1965 to 1970. A church that already occupied a position of prestige in its metropolitan area and in its denomination was discovering new life within its traditional structures. It was also experiencing fulfillment from its more diversified approach to the individual and corporate mission of its widely scattered congregation. The tension and anxiety caused by unrelenting experimentation was replaced by an inner peace which was rooted in a clear sense of direction for moving into the future.

10 Starting Again

During the course of refueling and checking the map, a few changes were made in the back seat of this imaginary automobile. Nelson had slipped out unobtrusively in order to begin his new assignment in Green Lake, Wisconsin. One month later on July 1, 1970, the Rev. Charles Thunn, who had served as associate minister since 1959 entered into "active retirement" in St. Petersburg, Florida. These two staff vacancies made it possible to consolidate the strengths of both ministries into a redefined job description for the next associate minister.

The impact of the strategic-planning process can be seen in the description of this staff position, especially the priority given to the parish zone plan. The combination of small-group ministry with more traditional pastoral visitation shows the new dimension which had been introduced during the later years of the experiment. The following job description was issued by the minister's cabinet on April 30, 1970, as a guide for the ministerial selection committee:

This individual should be seminary trained and ordained. He must be able to function effectively as a member of a three-man team and as an individual without supervision. He must be willing to innovate and should be an enabler, capable of motivating and training the laity for their ministry. The individual we seek must be mature and capable of identifying with all segments of our congregation. He should have teaching competence, although he will not be expected to take responsibility for our Christian education program. He must be supportive of Lake Avenue's definition of mission, which includes mission to its local urban neighborhood, its city-wide and suburban congregation, and, of course, the traditional world mission program.

Some specific areas of job responsibility are:

—Motivation and training of the congregation as a healing community engaged in reconciliation and mutual support.

—Staff leadership for further development and implementation of our parish zone plan.

—Development of additional small spiritual-quest groups within the membership.

—The development of special interest groups within the congregation by age, profession, special concern, etc.

—Special concern for pastoral care of the older segment of the congregation.

—Sharing of responsibility with other staff members for pastoral calling.

—Development of new member recruitment.

—Participation in the planning and execution of worship services, with occasional preaching opportunities.

The Rev. Roger H. Frances was called to fill this revised position of associate minister and began his ministry with the Lake Avenue Church in September of 1970. Exactly five years after the beginning of the experiment, the church was starting again with the new staff team of Hill, Pullis, and Frances.

Preventative Maintenance

The proper functioning of an automobile depends upon a regular schedule of preventative maintenance. The routine check of all the vital parts assures smooth, uninterrupted driving when starting out on a trip. One of the main lessons of the experiment was the intensified need to undergird the congregation with opportunities for maintenance of feelings and ideas in relation to one another.

In addition to the tension created by change and experimentation, a substantial portion of the congregation was irritated by Dr. George Hill's continual topical preaching on social justice. It was often misinterpreted by the laity and staff alike as a complete lack of concern for the many personal needs of people. The congregation felt like a forgotten people. Regarding this matter, Dr. Hill made the following comments during a taped interview with Lincoln in December of 1970:

As long as Jesus went about "doing good" (blessing little children, comforting the afflicted, speaking of the kingdom of God's love), he was warmly received and popularly acclaimed. But when he challenged the practices of the establishment through criticizing Pharisaic religion and banishing the money changers from the temple, the opposition coalesced and launched the conspiracy to do him in. The same situation constantly haunts any minister today. The call to goodness and charity wins friends, but presenting the claim of Christ for justice and righteousness mobilizes the enemy.

The contemporary pastor who attempts to be faithful to both the priestly and the prophetic dimensions of the gospel experiences something of the popularity-hostility syndrome in which Jesus was caught. Often the tensions created by prophetic proclamation in the pulpit must be assuaged by priestly ministrations in the privacy of home or study. Sometimes his prophetic stance in the pulpit will create such offense that the one who is threatened may become inaccessible to the priestly ministry of reconciliation. The temptation is always present here to "cool it" and thus become loved and accepted by everyone. But one makes this bargain only at the price of his integrity and his understanding of the fullness of the gospel.

For many church members prophetic preaching arouses feelings of guilt and frustration if it seems that the individual can do nothing about the problem. Community mission becomes an important part of the answer for those who take the prophetic word seriously. But when the church ventures out into mission, this route represents for many a disturbing change in the style of preaching and ministry. To the extent that Howard Moody is right when he declares that "the church exists for those who are not in it," this shift in direction from an essentially self-serving and introverted notion of the church's central purpose to one of recruiting and training for ministry with Christ in the world is often threatening to the traditionalist. Thus it becomes an imperative function of the minister to "run interference" for the new concept and practice of churchmanship and mission through theologically and biblically responsible preaching and teaching about the world for which Christ died and our responsibility with him for ministry in it. Moreover, while the church is trying to respond faithfully to its prophetic opportunity through mission by mobilizing all the human resources available for the task, it must in no sense neglect its priestly and supportive role among those who must lean upon the Christian community for strength and direction.

Our experiment in mission at Lake Avenue has produced several failures and a few successes, but, more importantly, it has introduced us to a style of ministry and churchmanship which will not be forgotten. In fact, our best insights and discoveries from the experiment are being incorporated into our long-range planning and our short-term goals. Our experience has convinced us that we are not really the church unless we are in prophetic mission together.

Few ministers argue so persuasively for the necessity of prophetic preaching *(kerygma)*, even at the expense of pastoral ministry. Yet the conflict between the two roles is minimized when a team ministry enables another member of the staff to emphasize pastoral ministry.

The end result of the experiment, above all else, was the revitalizing of pastoral ministry as a necessary ingredient for prophetic mission. In response to an inquiry from Lincoln, the new associate minister, Roger Frances, described the way in which he viewed his pastoral role at the Lake Avenue Church:

Real caring and humane relationships are what we are lacking and needing for the life of the church. Our families hunger for the opportunity to be together on the grounds of common interest, work, service, friendship, and outreach. The realization is dawning among a growing number of members that we must as families begin to show genuine interest in our fellow members. We must "find" one another again. Persons who show interest in the life of the Lake Avenue Church or those who have lapsed into an inactive status need the fleshly encounter with the body. Open persons who really enjoy meeting and getting to know others build and maintain healthy relationships which are essential and integral to the church in mission. This is no new thing. It's been going on in the life of this church in a limited and natural way for sometime and in some members from the beginning. Tragically, the natural and normative style of loving persons for themselves in the body has gotten lost or been obscured by the important functions of the church.

The discovery that the good news of *koinonia* can only be communicated by incarnation finds wider and wider acceptance. Couples are finding that their homes, by means of a supper and an evening together with *new* friends, offers a visible dimension of mission for them and permits them to consecrate at least their kitchen, dining, and living rooms for Christian ministry. This kind of concern is also a valid expression of the mutual ministry of the members of the congregation with each other.

The recovery of an authentic pastoral ministry for the church results from the integration of the life of the laity with the work of the clergy. We do not do separate things but function in specialized and complementary spheres. We share one ministry. Together we appreciate that the church cannot fulfill the redemptive task of bringing persons into humanizing relationships without the full participation of all.

Pastoral ministry set in the context of church renewal is the essential means of providing internal support for the congregation in mission. This is a necessary maintenance function, not of the status quo, but of the church on the go.

The Lake Avenue Church was now consciously trying to keep a balance between secular mission in the world and interpersonal maintenance in the church. It was hoped that the careful attention to preventative maintenance within the congregation would avoid the breakdown of communication and misunderstanding which would fragment the fellowship.

The combination of "prophet" and "priest" on the staff team was supplemented by an urban specialist whose primary responsibility was the equipping of God's people for mission in the world (diakonia). Claude Pullis constantly reminded the congregation of the wide gulf between actual performance and perpetuated image. His candid honesty as minister of education was an offense to many members. For example, he reported to the church's annual meeting in January of 1969 that in his opinion the congregation did not live up to the self-image that it was projecting to the denomination. In reflecting upon the actual situation following the five-year experiment, he described Lake Avenue Church as a congregation in creative tension.

It is a congregation in tension with itself; in tension between separated understandings of evangelism and mission; in tension between its understanding of community ministry and its participation in the universal misson of the church; in tension between its understanding of long-range planning and of new concepts mandating immediacy; in tension between understanding monetary mission support and self-giving through direct involvement; in tension between understanding a new evolving lay leadership and the more traditional style of churchmanship.

In spite of their diversity of gifts, he saw countless lay persons wanting to be used as integral tools of mission but who still remained spectators watching from the sidelines. For the most part the church had failed to utilize the laity's livelihood and talents for mission. He viewed the church's educational ministry as a mechanism for mobilizing the laity in mission and then for providing the necessary support to keep them involved. Attorneys, doctors, teachers, businessmen, musicians, contractors, and housewives needed to be recruited for mission in terms of their interests and capabilities. Unless the church helped the laity to take inventory of their own potentials, limitations, talents, and uniqueness, neither they nor the church would ever see the value of their humanness in relation to God's creation.

Although the church was at least marginally related to many new ministries, it seemed that only about 15 percent of its members were actually involved personally. It seemed initially that the majority of the congregation was geared to a late nineteenth-century liberalism which supported advocates of change but avoided direct action themselves. It is true that the argument of quality over quantity cannot negate the dynamic personal contribution of a few or the significant financial support of such projects by others. Yet this kind of quality can only be sustained if it attracts a sufficient number of sustainers. Quantity cannot denote quality, but quality without quantity could become weak. Weakness is synonymous with powerlessness. *Unless the church is a power base—a diverse coalition of large numbers of well-equipped persons ready to exert theological, personal, vocational, political, and economic influences, it cannot serve the world.* If viable ministries for a modern world are to continue, never mind flourish, the verbiage regarding a distinct dichotomy between quality and quantity must be significantly revised.

One of the disappointments of the experiment was the lack of significant increases in the number of persons involved in community mission or participating in worship, disciplined study, small-group experiences, or other supportive programs of the congregation. Yet part of the problem was the tendency to restrict true involvement to the newly developed community ministries either sponsored or enabled by the church.

When an inventory of mission involvement was taken in October of 1970, the entire church was astonished to learn that the "silent majority" of 85 percent were much more involved than any one had realized. The majority were related to volunteer associations, such as PTA, Red Cross, Scouts, and visiting corps to hospitals. Others expressed their faith through various political action groups concerned with world peace, civil rights, and environmental control. Naïve as it may sound, the Lake Avenue Church had never seriously legitimized these other involvements as mission activity, yet most of the congregation was involved in such activities.

Unfortunately it was not until the end of the experiment that such involvements in the wider metropolitan area were acknowledged as viable expressions of mission. An earlier step in this direction was the reorganization of the Women's Mission Society, but the overall impression given to the congregation was that mission to the community was the main priority. The initial response might be to think that a decentralized approach to lay ministry had been rationalized to cover such a broad range of activities so that commitment would be easier. What actually happened was that the church realized its responsibility to provide biblical and theological reference points for responsible living in a modern world. The church can also serve as an information resource, provide political stimulation, advocate dramatic social change, and even sponsor programs in which laity may or may not participate. But it must always be a respecter of personhood, an aviary for frustration, and a spiritual adrenalin bank.

By acknowledging secular activity as mission, the church acknowledged the world as part of creation and affirmed it as good even though it was troubled (cf. Genesis 1:31). Because the world is pluralistic, the church must be a center for dialogue, and it must provide a compass for reflecting upon nonactions. The church needs to acknowledge modern mission as interdisciplinary activity. The church must regard itself as being representative of the world— if not institutionally, then symbolically; if not in ethnic or economic composition, then in attitude. The church as part of the world is a gathering and dispersing of people from different circumstances as well as with different values and goals. Its people also have different problems and priorities, different concerns and commitments. In striving for total equality of all peoples the church must always be assertive, yet always be an agent for reconciliation. Commitment to Christ in our contemporary world often leads to conflict, but this tension usually results from a genuine concern for people. Only in the spirit of grace and forgiveness can energies coalesce against the causes of evil. Only then can there be diversity without division, disagreement without depersonalization, decision without damnation.

Lake Avenue Church has always been successful, but now it is putting the emphasis on obedience. What has helped most in its quest is a fuller appreciation for all people (even its own more traditional members) and the abolishment of a territorial concept which had everyone believing that the church's only concern was its immediate neighborhood. Such geographic isolation is common but nonetheless wrong; it encourages an attitude of exclusiveness. To be sure Lake Avenue Church is committed to staying in and serving its immediate community irrespective of the few parishioners who live there. But it now also sees more clearly the concerns of its larger parish: the personal and professional anxieties of its members, their interests and talents, inflation and unemployment, leisure time and automation, quality education and the arts, narcotics, ecology, and world peace. By encouraging all these dimensions to be aired, by assisting the laity to focus their attentions on what concerns them most, by providing some channels of activity and acknowledging with admiration the existence of others, a spirit of healing community is emerging.

Openness to the Future

The fact that the church is in the process of becoming indicates that there are unfulfilled areas in which further growth is still needed. The present emphasis is one of strengthening the congregational base in the midst of a complex maze of personal and corporate mission involvements. Because so much publicity was given to the new community projects in which about 15 percent of the congregation were involved, the other 85 percent rightly wondered about the value of their contribution. The minister's cabinet which was reactivated in March of 1968 responded to this situation by recommending that the main priority of the church for the next few years should be the realization of healing community. A comprehensive parish organization and experimental family clusters are in the process of being developed so that everyone's contribution to the church's total mission can be affirmed personally.

There is also a new mood of acceptance for occasional experiments with new forms of worship. Current modifications include more contemporary music and avant-garde banners creating an atmosphere of celebration. Families were asked to make each banner an expression of their corporate worship of God. They were first presented as an offering to the Christ child on Christmas Sunday of 1969. In addition to adding warmth and beauty to the sanctuary, they serve as a reminder of the freedom and spontaneity which is at the heart of the free church tradition. The younger families of the congregation are especially enthusiastic about this innovation. Major experimentation utilizing multimedia for worship and education has been prepared and is being implemented.

There is also a new spirit of reconciliation among those who were previously resistant to change. Church laity and staff actively pursued permanent funding through political action for WEDGE and for a day care center which will be located in the church. People of all ages freely embrace each other as an authentic expression of acceptance even though differing political opinions and value systems still prevail. Petitions are frequently circulated to gain support for a school desegregation, grade reorganization, reactivation of a police advisory board, construction of low-income housing projects, environmental control legislation, welfare reform, and peace in Southeast Asia. Increasing numbers are participating in political action groups. Why? Because Lake Avenue dared to be actively engaged in the world and finally allowed the world to enter the church, *but not without resistance, not without conflict.*

The renewal process which started in 1954 can be viewed statistically by looking at membership, attendance, and financial trends. The resident membership of 1,738 in 1954 has gradually declined to 1,172 in 1970, making a total loss of 566 during the past seventeen years. The average annual loss during this period was thirty-four members compared to an average annual loss of twenty-four members during the previous twenty-one years from 1934 (when the membership reached its peak of 2,255) to 1954. There has been no open conflict causing large numbers of members to leave the church. In spite of some differences of opinion with their ministers, the majority of those leaving simply found that it was more convenient to attend church nearer home where their children could be with their school friends. The majority of new members were either newcomers to the city who liked the church's program or the children of present members who were attending church school.

Although the average church attendance dropped from 840 in 1954 to 259 in 1970, some of the difference can be attributed to a change in method of counting in 1961 when the church school children were no longer included. The level of financial support has remained constant. The cost of living increase accounts for the budget difference between 1954 ($100,000) and 1970 ($136,-200). Nevertheless fewer members who are pledging the same budget indicate a higher level of commitment to the work of Christ through the congregation. The first year following the close of the experiment, the Lake Avenue Church met its increased budget with more ease than can be remembered in recent years. The initial debt of $370,000 for the building renovation of 1964 was being reduced rapidly. At a time when caution might be expected, it was a real affirmation of strength when the congregation pledged $90,000 for the World Mission Campaign in 1968. This is enough reason to speculate that the great tradition of missionary support in the past is still very much alive.

Throughout this report on church renewal, the process of institutional change in a particular congregation has been described as it actually happened. It is hoped that the hazards along the routes to mission in the world or ministry within the congregation will be helpful to other churches engaging in a similar quest. Some of the pitfalls are: the danger of choosing the wrong destination, the fear of altering routes, the danger of becoming sidetracked, the burden of excessive baggage, the unwillingness of some to give up the wheel, the reluctance of others to assume their responsibility to share in the driving, the neglect of vehicular maintenance, the aggravation of backseat passengers interested only in the ride, the refusal of some to pay the toll, and so on. The process of completing the analogies would be a good exercise for those who wish to use the Lake Avenue Church experiment as the basis for evaluating their own situation.

It might appear that the Lake Avenue Church has all the answers. Hardly! This church is the first to admit that the experiment actually accomplished very little of what was aspired or even expected (see chapter 2). On the one hand, the effort became an experiment in community renewal of a neighborhood with limited yet significant results. On the other hand, the experiment was prophetic and preparatory for the congregation.

In "starting again," not over, the Lake Avenue Church accepted the recommendations of the long-range planning committee as a mandate to be in the process of continual renewal. In order to deal more effectively and personally with conflict, church leaders are determined to remember the lessons already learned. One of their concerns is with a road hazard too often ignored, the *pothole of pride* which is especially dangerous in a church which is blessed with considerable affluence. Perhaps the best corrective is the spirit of prayer which was conveyed by Dr. George Hill during a regular worship service on October 17, 1965, at the beginning of the five-year experiment.

O God, our gracious, loving, and heavenly Father, thou who in thy wisdom didst summon us into the fellowship of Jesus Christ, and into the life and ministry of his church, we come before thee as thy children. We come not because we are better than those outside thy church, not because we are more deserving of thy love, not because by the excellence of our lives or the clearness of our own testimony do we deserve thy love in a special way. We come simply as an act of obedience to Jesus Christ. We come simply because we have discovered our own inner need for the sustaining fellowship of his church. We come into thy presence proclaiming our weakness and our imperfection, our frailty and our sin. We do this gladly, because we have learned to rely upon thy gracious love, thy tender and forgiving Spirit. We thank thee, our Father, that we are not called to stand before thee because of what we are, but we come into thy presence without hesitation because we know that thou art Love and Forgiveness. We pray that as we come into thy presence we may become ever clearer in our understanding of the nature of our ministry to one another, and to those to whom the church is sent.

Forgive us, O God, when the church speaks only to itself. Help us to dedicate our lives, our talents, our creativity to getting the message and the ministry of the church into the world, the world for which Christ lived and died, the world to which we are committed as obedient and faithful servants. God grant that we may have the wisdom and the self-discipline to learn to know that world, to break down all protective isolation and insulation from its pain, its restlessness, its despair, its stark need. Give us the mind of Christ. Help us to look upon that world in his spirit and through his eyes, to lay his claims before it, to give ourselves to it and for it, even as Christ gave himself to it and for it. Deliver us from a preoccupation with ourselves and with nice people like us. Help us to go forth as servants of the most high God, not ministering simply to one another in the closed society of the little church, but willing to venture forth with Christ into paths of useful, creative and responsible mission. We pray that thou wilt help us come to know and understand and love our neighbors, so that we do not have to speak of them in vague, impersonal, far-off terms. Help us to know them and love them, and thus to seek to minister with them. To this task we offer ourselves, and we pray that thou wilt sustain us, through Jesus Christ our Lord.

In this spirit the church continues with new leadership. After seventeen years of significant service to the Lake Avenue Church, Dr. Hill accepted the call to become senior minister of the Calvary Baptist Church, Washington, D. C. Yet the journey toward renewal initiated during his Rochester pastorate left the Lake Avenue Church with clearly defined routes for urban mission in the community and mutual ministry within the congregation.

New Routes for Old Churches—Guidelines for Group Discussion

The next step is the application of the renewal process to the particular needs of your church.

The first step after choosing a destination is to discover the possible routes leading to that particular destination. Depending upon the purpose of the trip, a route is finally chosen. If the trip is to be a leisurely sightseeing tour, then the scenic route would be chosen. However, if time is limited, it would be important to take the most direct route. Each church is unique and must seek guidance in determining which route or routes are appropriate to its situation. The following guidelines are aimed at helping you to apply the findings of this report to the problems and opportunities confronted by your congregation. The continuation of the automobile analogy will accentuate the variety of options which may be considered in an authentic process of institutional change aimed at discovering wholeness of ministry.

CHAPTER 1: Who Is in the Driver's Seat?

The various roles played by professional and lay leadership of a congregation may be studied in order to determine where the pressure for change will likely originate. At the Lake Avenue Church a key layman was the initial change agent who persisted in making himself a nuisance. The key professional staff member was most helpful in preparing a climate for change and in interpreting the new developments to the congregation. He welcomed and accepted those lay persons who chose to sit with him in the driver's seat. Later he trusted them enough to move to the back seat.

—Where is the pressure for change coming from in your congregation?

 —Restless Youth
 —Searching Adults

—Aggressive Clergy

—How does your minister demonstrate that he is secure enough to risk turning over the driver's seat to lay leadership?

—To what extent have your lay leaders gained the respect of your minister on the basis of their biblical and theological perspective?

—How important is it for your minister to be free enough to relate in depth to at least a few people?

—Who will have to take the initiative if a genuine team ministry is to develop between the professional and lay leadership of your congregation?

CHAPTER 2:
What Can Be Learned from Our Past Driving Record?

The history of a congregation may be studied in order to determine the previous rate of change. The Lake Avenue Church has been in a steady period of membership decline since 1934. Yet the congregation resisted the pressure to relocate in the suburbs and *chose* to engage in a challenging urban ministry. The willingness to experiment with community ministry on a small scale indicated a style of congregational life that was open to an orderly process of change.

—To what extent is your congregation controlled by conformity to traditions of the past?

—How seriously does your congregation take a pattern of membership decline which might point to the need for change?

—Are the changes that you would like to make aimed at institutional survival or more faithful service?

—What is the most concrete way that your congregation could show concern for the people in your immediate neighborhood?

—How would you evaluate your congregation's willingness to engage in experimentation on the basis of Christian love, whether or not it results in additions to the church membership?

CHAPTER 3: Which Route Should We Take?

The decision of the Lake Avenue Church to remain in the city and renovate its facilities was like giving priority to the route of urban mission. The implications of the decision were so uncertain that considerable time and energy went into studying the main landmarks which could be expected on this route. A few clergy-men eventually jumped in the driver's seat and took off on the route of ecumenical cooperative ministry.

—What connection do you see between the exploration of mission and an authentic renewal process?
—Which aspect of mission is more difficult for your congregation?
  —The immediate community
  —The larger community
  —The nation
  —The world community
—What are the areas of investigation that will help you to understand most fully your immediate community?
  —Population trends
  —Social and economic characteristics
  —Religious affiliations
—What kind of program could the church sponsor which would respond to one urgent need in this neighborhood?
—Who are the opinion leaders who could most easily initiate this program?

CHAPTER 4: With Whom Should We Travel?

The openness to change was not limited to the Lake Avenue Church but was shared by other congregations. This cooperative approach made it possible for more to be accomplished in a short period of time than could have happened in a unilateral approach. Both clergy and laity took turns driving as the strain of the trip became more evident.

—How much does doctrinal agreement influence your willingness to work with other Christians?
—Would you have to give up anything in order to engage in cooperative planning and programming in which no one church is able to dominate?
—How would you feel if called upon to serve in a mission project which put you in a team relationship with other Protestants or Catholics to whom you would be accountable?
—To what extent would you be willing to accept those who disagreed with this kind of cooperative approach?
—What evidence would you look for in determining whether an experimental program should end or continue to exist?

CHAPTER 5: How Flexible Are Our Plans?

Just when everything was going fine with church-sponsored mission projects, a forgotten neighborhood was discovered which was intimidated by church control. The high-speed traffic on the main route was not even aware that it was "passing by on the other side" and ignoring those who were in greatest need.

—To what extent do we choose to minister to and with those who are most like us?

—How can we get to know those who are different without seeming to be superior?

—Can you recall an experience in which you were actually helped by a person that you were seeking to help?

—How wide is the socioeconomic range of your congregation?

—What would you have to do in order to make a broader range of people more comfortable in your church?

CHAPTER 6: Where Are the Most Dangerous Intersections?

It was quite natural that the cooperating churches should align themselves with Edgerton Area neighborhood residents, most of whom happened to be property owners. At the same time they were becoming aware of tenants and welfare recipients in Brown Square who were interested in self-determination. The Lake Avenue Church was caught in the middle of a dangerous intersection between the powerful majority of home owners and the powerless minority that lived in substandard housing. This precarious position was the cause of considerable anxiety both in the church and in its immediate community.

—How can your congregation affirm property owners and politicians whose primary goal is to preserve and improve their common neighborhood?

—How would you distinguish between genuine community and political patronage?

—What are the potential areas for conflict of interest between your church and its immediate community?

—Can all problems of social change be dealt with on an individual basis, or is it more likely that self-determination will take place in an organization with others who are seeking to help themselves?

—Can you recall an experience in which you were forced to grow because of a conflict situation that could not be avoided?

CHAPTER 7: Will the Rights of Other Drivers Be Respected?

As the Lake Avenue Church became more aware of its untenable position, its main loyalty shifted to the tenants and welfare recipients who were searching for another vehicle which would take them on the route of indigenous self-determination. This shift meant that it would be necessary to respect the rights of other drivers and, whenever necessary, to offer to ride along in the back seat.

—Which group in your community is the least involved in the decision making about its future destiny?

—How can you express concern for this group without appearing to exercise control?

—Illustrate what it would mean to receive love from those who are less fortunate than you instead of just giving it to them?

—Can you recall any situation in which basic human rights were given to a powerless group because of the generosity of benevolent citizens?

—What steps could your congregation take to demonstrate concern for helping the poor to organize so that they can negotiate for their rights and be negotiated with from a position of equality?

CHAPTER 8: From Whom Do We Get Our Directions?

The danger of any apparent advance in mission is that man will attribute the progress to his engineering skill and organizational ability. Yet the more involved the Lake Avenue Church became, the more earnestly its members sought direction from God. The strategy of this search for divine guidance was the formation of small groups. Learning to listen to God and to one another was much more difficult than listening to the conflicting voices of neighborhood residents, whether they were property owners or tenants.

—How do your official boards seek to create a climate in which the members can relate at the level of personal faith?

—What meaning does prayer have in your congregation beyond providing a religious formality for calling a meeting to order?

—How seriously are the professional and lay leaders of your congregation being challenged by personal Bible study in which the emphasis is on God's plan for your life and your church?

—To what extent do the members of your congregation find a sense of belonging by relating in depth to at least a few significant others?

—What steps could your congregation take to strengthen the resources of its inner life?

CHAPTER 9: How Far Ahead Should We Go?

The tension between external involvement in mission and the inner resources of Christian community created a situation in which priorities had to be determined. At the Lake Avenue Church it was decided that wholeness of ministry had been distorted in favor of public involvement at the expense of interpersonal relationships. Therefore, the emphasis for the next few years was placed on the need for healing community. It was decided to overemphasize the decentralized approach to urban mission so that the majority of the congregation could be affirmed in relation to mission opportunities that were accessible throughout the metropolitan area.

—What is the strength of your congregation which could distort wholeness of ministry?

   —Proclamation

   —Fellowship

   —Service

—What is the weakest area of your congregation which needs reinforcement in order to provide a more balanced ministry?

—How can you engage in a process of orderly change aimed at discovering wholeness without leaving many members behind?

—Who should belong to a strategic-planning group in your church if it is to be representative of all segments in your congregation?

—How would you begin to evaluate your present ministry in order to determine short-range and long-range goals for the future?

CHAPTER 10: What Is Our Destination?

The lasting contribution of the experiment at the Lake Avenue Church was in bringing professional and lay leaders together at a deeper level of mutual trust and joint planning for the future ministry of the congregation. No longer was the major emphasis of the church just a general response to the latest crisis in the city. It was also an orderly process of institutional change in which many members were finding support for a great diversity of mission opportunities. At the same time some were discovering new levels of personal commitment to Christ and deeper experiences of Christian community.

— How realistic is it to expect that your church will be able to develop equal competence in proclaiming the gospel, in becoming a supportive community, and in demonstrating Christian service to others?

— Is it any more likely that this kind of wholeness will come from a group of churches that are able to share their strengths with each other?

— What has your experience been in seeking to give expression to this kind of wholeness in a small group in which a variety of gifts are shared?

— How do you respond to the challenge that God expects every church to be in the process of becoming a more faithful expression of the gospel?

— To what extent has a climate of change been created in your church through which God can work out his purpose of reconciliation for all men through Christ?